VALUING AND SELLING YOUR BUSINESS

A QUICK GUIDE TO CASHING IN

Tim McDaniel

apress®

Valuing and Selling Your Business: A Quick Guide to Cashing In

Copyright © 2014 by Tim McDaniel

This work is subject to copyright. All rights are reserved by the Publisher, whether the whole or part of the material is concerned, specifically the rights of translation, reprinting, reuse of illustrations, recitation, broadcasting, reproduction on microfilms or in any other physical way, and transmission or information storage and retrieval, electronic adaptation, computer software, or by similar or dissimilar methodology now known or hereafter developed. Exempted from this legal reservation are brief excerpts in connection with reviews or scholarly analysis or material supplied specifically for the purpose of being entered and executed on a computer system, for exclusive use by the purchaser of the work. Duplication of this publication or parts thereof is permitted only under the provisions of the Copyright Law of the Publisher's location, in its current version, and permission for use must always be obtained from Springer. Permissions for use may be obtained through RightsLink at the Copyright Clearance Center. Violations are liable to prosecution under the respective Copyright Law.

ISBN-13 (pbk): 978-1-4842-0845-8

ISBN-13 (electronic): 978-1-4842-0844-1

Trademarked names, logos, and images may appear in this book. Rather than use a trademark symbol with every occurrence of a trademarked name, logo, or image we use the names, logos, and images only in an editorial fashion and to the benefit of the trademark owner, with no intention of infringement of the trademark.

The use in this publication of trade names, trademarks, service marks, and similar terms, even if they are not identified as such, is not to be taken as an expression of opinion as to whether or not they are subject to proprietary rights.

While the advice and information in this book are believed to be true and accurate at the date of publication, neither the authors nor the editors nor the publisher can accept any legal responsibility for any errors or omissions that may be made. The publisher makes no warranty, express or implied, with respect to the material contained herein.

>Managing Director: Welmoed Spahr
>Acquisitions Editor: Jeff Olson
>Developmental Editor: Robert Hutchinson
>Editorial Board: Steve Anglin, Mark Beckner, Gary Cornell, Louise Corrigan, James DeWolf, Jonathan Gennick, Robert Hutchinson, Michelle Lowman, James Markham, Matthew Moodie, Jeff Olson, Jeffrey Pepper, Douglas Pundick, Ben Renow-Clarke, Gwenan Spearing, Matt Wade, Steve Weiss
>Coordinating Editor: Rita Fernando
>Copy Editor: Jennifer Sharpe
>Compositor: SPi Global
>Indexer: SPi Global
>Cover Designer: Anna Ishchenko

Distributed to the book trade worldwide by Springer Science+Business Media New York, 233 Spring Street, 6th Floor, New York, NY 10013. Phone 1-800-SPRINGER, fax (201) 348-4505, e-mail orders-ny@springer-sbm.com, or visit www.springeronline.com. Apress Media, LLC is a California LLC and the sole member (owner) is Springer Science + Business Media Finance Inc (SSBM Finance Inc). SSBM Finance Inc is a Delaware corporation.

For information on translations, please e-mail rights@apress.com, or visit www.apress.com.

Apress and friends of ED books may be purchased in bulk for academic, corporate, or promotional use. eBook versions and licenses are also available for most titles. For more information, reference our Special Bulk Sales–eBook Licensing web page at www.apress.com/bulk-sales.

Any source code or other supplementary materials referenced by the author in this text is available to readers at www.apress.com. For detailed information about how to locate your book's source code, go to www.apress.com/source-code/.

Father, thank you for your amazing grace.
Sola Gratia!

Foreword

"What is my business worth?" "How do I know I am getting the right price?" "Isn't my company worth more?" "Why can't I get money for all those years I worked so hard?" "Isn't my sweat and blood worth more?"

These are only a few of the many difficult questions business owners ask when thinking about selling their "baby"—the company. Unfortunately, owners often believe the company is worth far more than the actual or true value of the company. Owners are obviously emotional when it comes to thinking about selling. It is only natural. Based on over 35 years of assisting business owners sell and buy companies, I have experienced how stressful a sale can be on the owner, and how ill-prepared many owners are as they prepare for the big event. Knowing what the buyer wants, completing a detailed exercise in due diligence, doing the groundwork . . . are all stressful. Experienced attorneys and accountants can help manage these tasks and reduce the stress. However, recognizing and accepting the actual value of the company may be the greatest stress of all—because owners believe their baby is the most attractive of all!

Luckily, Tim McDaniel, an experienced business valuator, has presented help for owners contemplating a sale. He can assist owners understand the "actual value" of the company, and provide suggestions on how to grow its value.

Whenever Tim is involved with my clients, I know they will understand the process and the valuation conclusion. I am always pleased to introduce Tim to clients because he does a great job explaining issues in plain English without complicated statistics or formulas. His perspective on valuations is much wider than mathematical formulas, high finance, or theories.

Tim's experience in the M&A transaction world is the basis of his sophisticated view. Best of all, he brings a human touch. Tim is diligent in truly understanding what clients want, and he takes a holistic approach when discussing client exit strategies.

In short, Tim has the ability to incorporate a client's personal desires with the realities of the current situation.

So often, valuations are totally incomprehensible to owners. But owners of businesses who read this book will understand fully the importance of looking at their business like an investment. They will be grateful for Tim's insight.

—Beatrice E. Wolper, President
Emens & Wolper Law Firm

About the Author

Tim McDaniel is a shareholder at Rea & Associates, Inc., a large regional public accounting firm. McDaniel directs the business valuation and succession planning practice for the firm. He has over 23 years of experience and has been involved in over 2,000 valuation and planning engagements. He also provided services in the firm's former M&A transaction practice, giving him significant real-world experience to pass on to his clients. McDaniel prides himself on being able to teach business owners in everyday language how to value their most prized asset—their company. He shows them practical ways to increase the value of their business and how to successfully exit their business on their terms.

He is a certified public accountant and the author of nearly 40 articles in publications like *CPA Voice*, *American Venture Magazine*, and *Valuation Strategies*. He has obtained the top three professional valuation credentials (ASA, CBA, ABV). He is also an active national speaker on valuation, exit strategies, and succession planning, and he has served an expert witness in over two dozen cases.

McDaniel lives in Westerville, Ohio with his wife, April, and his three children, Drew, Elle, and Charlie.

Acknowledgments

I would like to thank Apress and their amazing team for providing me with this opportunity. I have such a passion to teach business owners about the valuation of their business, how to make it more valuable, and how to cash in the fruits of their labor by selling their business. I am grateful for Apress that made it possible to express this passion in this book.

I would like to thank my colleagues and partners at Rea & Associates, Inc. I am very fortunate to be working with a group of men and women who are bright and compassionate people. This book would not be possible without their support over the years.

Most importantly, I would like to thank my wife and children. Without their patience and willingness to sacrifice, this book would still be a dream. To April, Drew, Elle, and Charlie, thank you for your love and patience. You all are such a blessing to me, and I am a very lucky man to have each one of you in my life.

Introduction

A quick guide to cashing in! It would be awesome if selling your business and living happily ever after was quick and easy. It is not. Do not let the subtitle of the book fool you. The subtitle is in reference to the type of book this is rather than how easy it is to value and sell your business.

This book is written to the business owner that wants a quick read about the valuation and selling process in an easy-to-read format. My goal is for you to be able to know how your business is valued, be aware of ways to grow that value, and understand the selling process in less than four hours.

My ideas are intended to be understandable, straightforward, and direct. This book is not written for the professionals who serve the business owner but it is written directly to you—the business owner.

If you want to maximize your personal wealth it is important that you understand the valuation and selling process.

There are two disturbing trends that I see with many of my clients. The first is a major disconnect between the actual business value and the owner's perception of that value. The second trend I see is that, even though in most situations a business owner's largest financial asset is his or her business, he or she does not view it as an actual asset or investment. My clients when they come to me have been spending considerable time and money with their investment advisors growing their stock and bond portfolios, while putting no effort into knowing and growing the value of their largest assets—their businesses.

Once I noticed these trends, I started to recognize the major consequences that the business owners were having in not treating their businesses as investments. I was convinced that if business owners simply changed their mindset and started to treat their businesses as investments, they would have a greater sense of purpose and become wealthier. This discovery started my journey of preaching to all business owners that they need to treat their businesses as investments. Treating your business as an investment includes knowing its true value, having a plan to grow that value, and understanding how to realize the value that is in your business through a sale. If you can walk away from this book fully understanding the valuation process, knowing how to increase the value of your business, and understanding the selling process, then reading this book was well worth your time.

Introduction

I cannot guarantee that reading this book will double or triple the value of your business in five years. The business world is complex, and you obviously don't have total control of your destiny. You can take all the advice in this book and still not have things turn out the way you want. However, when you gain knowledge and take action, your chance of being successful increases.

I derived and adapted this book from a self-standing portion of my previous book, *Know and Grow the Value of Your Business: An Owner's Guide to Retiring Rich.* In *Valuing and Selling Your Business: A Quick Guide to Cashing In,* I focus on selling one's business as an exit strategy—to the exclusion of the various other exit strategies covered in my longer work, such as gifting to the next generation, retaining the business, and liquidation. In addition, my previous book includes more in-depth discussion about treating your business as an investment, more decision-making tools, and more examples. If you are unsure of what your exit strategy should be and what your full range of options is, please read *Know and Grow the Value of Your Business.*

The appendices in the present book detail what is required in a valuation repor and show you samples of the documentation that buyers will request from you when you sell your business. Although this book was not written to make you a valuation expert, you will find it instructive to see what is included in a valuation report. This is why I've included an excerpt of the AICPA business valuation standards. In case you need to have a valuation prepared for a third party such as the IRS, the AICPA excerpt in the final appendix provides reporting guidelines for business valuations and a comprehensive glossary of terms.

The sample due diligence request in the appendix will also be of great benefit to you. It gives you a head's-up of what your potential buyer will request and serves as a checklist to make sure you assemble all the proper documentation and items that you will need for a buyer.

Thank you for picking up this book. After reading it, you will look at your business differently, I hope—seeing it as your most important financial investment. Finally, my fervent wish is that it helps you to "cash in" on the many years of blood, sweat, and tears you have put into your business!

CHAPTER 1

Country Club Lifestyle
Do You Know Your Value?

A sophisticated businesswoman in her sixties called me late one summer afternoon. "Mr. McDaniel, I would like you to value my company in order to complete a transaction with my nephew." We spoke further and arranged a meeting for the following week. When I arrived at her company, I noticed how nice the furnishings were. It had the appearance of a very successful company. She provided me a tour and explained how the company started, her role in the business, and other relevant facts that were needed to prepare a business valuation. She explained to me that she was selling the business to her nephew, who worked in the company. He was in his late twenties and had been in the business for about six years.

I had seen numerous engagements like this one—a client wanting to use an independent valuator to set the price between related parties. It is required by the Internal Revenue Service (IRS),[1] and it often saves some bad blood between relatives down the road.

However, I was very surprised to find out that this engagement was different. When I asked her if my services and valuation report would be used to set the purchase price, she replied, "Oh no, the price is set. We just need a valuation report in order for my nephew to obtain a bank loan." I asked,

---

[1] Transactions between related parties need to be at "fair market value," or they may be considered a gift by the IRS and thus taxable.

"What is the price?" She said, "$2.5 million." I continued, "How did you determine that price?" Without hesitation, she said, "This is the amount I need to support my country club lifestyle. I belong to an exclusive country club and if I obtained $2.5 million, I will be able to maintain my membership at this club and live the lifestyle I want." I was stunned by her answer. At that point in my career, I had been involved in more than 1,000 valuation engagements and never had a client provide an answer like that.

I proceeded with the engagement and determined that the company was worth significantly less than her expectations. It was my opinion that the company was valued at about one-third of her expectations—only $800,000. Besides the $50,000 salary that the nephew received from the company, he had no other financial resources and no bank would provide him with an $800,000 loan, let alone a $2.5 million loan.

How could this very smart businesswoman be so wrong? Why did she wait until she was in her sixties to find this out? Unfortunately, to maintain her country club lifestyle, she would have to continue working or find a fool who would grossly overpay at $2.5 million.

Her compensation from her business was $250,000, enough to provide her with the lifestyle she wanted. There was only one catch. She had to go to the office each day and work hard to make sure that her customers were happy, the employees were doing their jobs, and the bills were paid. If she would have sold her business at the true fair market value, she would have received close to $600,000 after paying taxes and transaction fees. Like most business owners, her business interest was about 75% of her net worth. With her spending habits, the proceeds from the sale of her business would provide her with the lifestyle she wanted for only a few years.

While no one had ever told me they arrived at a price based on the country club lifestyle they desired to have, the details here are commonplace. Business owners guess at what their business is worth (their most important asset), and they typically guess wrong. Unfortunately, their guesswork leads to undesirable consequences such as:

- Being unable to retire at the lifestyle they expect
- Working more years than they had hoped
- Choosing the wrong time to sell their business
- Not being able to exit their business on their own terms

What if the client had known that her business was only worth $800,000 when she was 55 instead of 63? She could have implemented strategies to increase the value of her business and then lived the lifestyle she wanted.

Alternatively, she could have changed her lifestyle to fit the actual proceeds she would receive when she sold her business. But now, it was going to be very difficult for her to remedy the situation at age 63.

Important There are major consequences to you and your future in guessing wrong at the value of your business.

Treat Your Business Like an Investment

The majority of the net worth of most business owners is tied up in the value of their business. It is their most important investment, but it is rare that they view it this way. Business owners spend more time and money managing liquid assets (stocks, bonds, and mutual funds), which are easy to value and do not have the large potential for growth like their business does. Typical business owners do not view their business as an "investment." It is more of a "piggy bank," "identity," or "a job."

Treating your business as an investment is critical for you to accomplish your long-term financial goals and increasing your net worth.

Your business is no different than your other investments. Small changes in the annual rate of return will have a large impact on the future value of the investment. The major difference between your business investment and your other investments is that the business is a much larger part of your overall net worth. Growth in the value of your business will have a greater impact on your net worth than the growth in your other investments. Consider this example.

Elle owns a business, and she has a total net worth of $5 million. Her net worth consists of the following assets:

- Value of the business: $3 million
- Marketable securities: $1 million
- Real estate and other assets: $1 million

She reads the *Wall Street Journal* on a daily basis and has quarterly meetings with her investment advisor to discuss her marketable securities portfolio. Her goal is to earn a 7% annual return on her marketable securities over the next ten years and then retire. If she achieves her goal, the securities will be worth $1.97 million. If there is no growth in the value of her business and other assets, her net worth would grow to $5.97 million.

Now let's assume that she is also focused on growing the value of her business at the same 7% rate over the next ten years. If she achieves her goal, the business will be worth $5.90 million. If both the business and marketable securities investments grow at 7% annually, her net worth would grow to be $8.87 million in ten years.

By focusing on growing her business along with the value of her securities, Elle's net worth will be $2.9 million higher ten years from now.

How can you treat your business like the important investment that it is? In order to treat your business like an investment, you must take the following steps:

- Know the true value of your business.
- Have specific plans to increase its value.
- A plan to realize value "cash in" through a sale of the business.

Your business is every bit as much an investment as stocks, bonds, and mutual funds. Treating your business like an investment is the key to increasing value and building wealth.

Most business owners have a vague sense of the selling price for their business. It is usually in terms of the amount they believe they need to live the rest of their lives comfortably without working. Not much thought is given to who the best buyer for their business is and when is the best time to sell their business. These business owners usually sell their business at a price much lower than they anticipated and at times are forced to sell their business due to life circumstances,

I have met very few business owners who actually have specific written plans to grow the value of their business and know the importance of having their business in its sellable position at all times in order to provide them with the best opportunity of selling their business at the right price and the right time. The business owners that actively work these specific plans are able to move on to their next phase of life on their terms.

Summary

It is critical that you actually know what your business is worth. Guessing at its value based on your personal needs will lead you down the wrong path. It is important to have an "investment mindset" towards your business. It is your most valuable asset and, by focusing on growing this asset and having a plan to realize value from a sale, you can increase your net worth significantly.

In the next chapter, you will learn more about what a business valuation is and who is qualified to prepare one. By the end of Chapter 4, you should have a solid understanding of the entire business valuation process and how to increase the value of your business.

CHAPTER 2

Valuation Fundamentals

Valuation in Plain English

"I don't want to pay that much for a valuation," the caller said. "Can't you just put my numbers into the computer and spit out my value? I just want something quick and dirty." This is an all-too-common conversation that I have with potential clients. The truth is, there's no such thing as a quick valuation, and there's no (reputable) computer program that can provide an accurate valuation based on a bunch of numbers you input.

In this chapter, I will explain the entire valuation process by using everyday language. So if you are a valuation professional, please forgive me for not using the specific nomenclature that you are used to.

Let's look at a real-life example that shows why a good valuation depends on much more than looking at only financial records. There is a national parts distributor that buys products directly from manufacturers and then processes and repackages the products and delivers them to the retailer. The retailer then sells the products to the consumer. Historically, the distributor's revenues have been over $100 million and the annual profits have been consistently over $4 million.

How much is this business worth? Should it be based on a percentage of revenues? How about a multiple of earnings?

The actual value of this business is less than $1 million. How can this be? Based on historical earnings, you would earn the purchase price in three months. What a bargain! Interested?

Chapter 2 | Valuation Fundamentals

The rest of the story is that the distributor is very dependent on one customer. That customer accounts for over $90 million (or 90%) of the $100 million in annual sales. They recently lost the customer and may liquidate the business rather than try to rebuild it. After selling the company's assets and paying off all the company's obligations, the owner believes that he will be able to put just less than $1 million into his pocket. This process will take a couple of years.

Would you get the right answers if you simply put numbers into a spreadsheet and based the value on historical earnings? Absolutely not! Why? It's because of the following point:

Important Valuation is a prophecy of the future based on the information that the valuator has as of the valuation date.

If someone has prepared a valuation for you by using a canned valuation software program without interviewing you and without understanding your business and industry, please take the valuation report and throw it in the trash. It's not worth your time.

The valuation process is a mystery for most business owners. Web sites, articles, and books like this one can shed light on the mechanics of placing a value on a business and will provide you with some education on how to value a business. However, the terms used in many of these resources makes the valuation process seem more complex than it actually is.

Some business owners will hear stories from their friends or read articles about how much money others have received from selling their business. "It was simple," says the friend. "They gave me five times earnings." This makes the valuation process seem easy.

The reality is that the valuation process is much more involved than multiplying an earnings number by a multiplier, but it is not so complex that you cannot understand it.

Hopefully after reading this chapter, you will have a basic understanding of the valuation process and be able to explain to your spouse in plain English this process. You will also know the difference between *enterprise value*, *equity value*, and the *net proceeds* that you receive after you sell your business. The discussion is still more of an overview, but a necessary one. In the next chapter, we will dive in deeper and provide more of a "how the sausage is made" explanation of the valuation process.

What Is a Business Valuation?

A business valuation is a process and a set of procedures used to estimate the value of an owner's interest in a business. The key words in this definition are process, procedures, and estimate.

A long-standing resource that describes business valuation and the important factors in the valuation process is IRS Revenue Ruling 59-60 (usually known as 59-60). When it was introduced in 1959, 59-60 was the most important resource in determining how to value a business. It has stood the test of time and continues to provide a guide to business valuators on how to prepare a valuation for the IRS and for other purposes. The following is a key excerpt from 59-60:

> *Valuation of securities is, in essence, a prophecy as to the future and must be based on facts available at the required date of appraisal.*

Let's break down this definition further. Valuation is an *estimate* of value. Of the 2,000+ valuation engagements that I have been involved in, there have been only a handful of times that an actual sale of the appraised business occurred within a few months of the valuation date. Almost 100% of the time, I had no verification of how close my estimate of value would be to reality. In part, that's because many are done for estate planning purposes, divorces, and other efforts that do not involve the sale of the business.

I'll be the first to say that valuations are subjective. The IRS concurs, to a degree. The opening paragraph of 59-60 states the following:

> *In valuing the stock of closely held corporations, or the stock of corporations where market quotations are not available, all other available financial data, as well as all relevant factors affecting the fair market value must be considered for estate tax and gift tax purposes. No general formula may be given that is applicable to the many different valuation situations arising in the valuation of such stock. However, the general approach, methods, and factors which must be considered in valuing such securities are outlined.*

How do you know if the conclusion is correct? Unfortunately, you don't. And this is where the next part of the definition is important. *There are recognized processes and procedures that are standard in the business valuation industry.*

Therefore, a business valuation is much more than simply putting numbers into a spreadsheet and spitting out a number. If a valuation is an estimate based on a prophecy of the future, how is this done? With a crystal ball? Dartboard? Truthfully, these may provide you with more insight than an analysis prepared by untrained professionals using computerized software.

Chapter 2 | Valuation Fundamentals

Before we dive into the recognized processes and procedures of a business valuation, let's discuss the business valuation profession and when a business valuation is needed.

The Valuation Profession

When you need a business valuation, where should you go? To your CPA who prepares a few valuations a year, aided by his latest and greatest software program? To an Internet provider that promises you cheap and fast valuations? Or what about those professionals who travel around the country leading slick seminars that will get you all enthused about selling your business? Of course, those "professionals" also want you to sign up for only a $55,000 business valuation to start the process.

So how do you decide who will prepare the valuation of your business?

Business valuation has become its own profession. There are four major professional organizations that provide training and accreditation to the business valuation profession. For each one, the accreditation process includes testing on valuation theory and standards, submission of work product, and an experience requirement. Some designations are harder to obtain than others (e.g., ASA); however, if someone has a designation from one of the following four organizations, you can know that the valuator understands the recognized processes and procedures used in a business valuation:

- ASA (Accredited Senior Appraiser) by the American Society of Appraisers
- ABV (Accredited in Business Valuation) by the American Institute of Certified Public Accountants.
- CVA (Certified Valuation Analyst) by the National Association of Certified Valuators and Analysts
- CBA (Certified Business Appraiser) by the Institute of Business Appraisers

A business valuation incorporates many different disciplines and requires the valuator to have a variety of skill sets. Valuators or their teams need to be familiar with the following in order to produce a credible business valuation:

- Know how to read financial statements and understand accounting theory.
- Understand how income taxes impact value.
- Know the relevant tax codes and court cases on valuation issues.

- Be able to perform robust financial analyses.
- Understand how the economy will impact a business's cash flow.
- Have a firm grasp of valuation theory and be able to apply the appropriate valuation methods.
- Be able to research complex issues.
- Know how publicly traded stocks are valued.
- Be able to communicate the results of a valuation to a business owner, a judge, or the IRS.

In addition to these skills, the valuator needs to apply "common sense" and be unbiased. At the end of the day, the valuator should step back and ask the question: "Would I buy the business at the price I valued it?" At times, it is clear to me that a valuator's conclusion is not remotely close to the actual value. This is typically due to a valuator's lack of knowledge or experience, or a decision to provide a biased opinion of value. At times, business valuators can become advocates and manipulate the results in order to please their client.

It will be difficult for you to determine the skill and the common sense of the business valuator. So how do you objectively hire the right person for you? Of course, I am biased, but I suggest that you look for the following when hiring a business valuator:

- It should be a full-time profession and not something they do occasionally to supplement their income.
- They should have at least two designations from the organizations listed previously.
- Experience is a critical factor, similar to choosing a surgeon. You don't want your company to be one of the valuator's first projects. You should select someone who has been involved with hundreds of valuation projects.
- They should be able to explain complex business issues to you in plain English. They should also be willing to sit down with you and your family members and explain how the valuation was prepared and why they chose a certain conclusion. You want someone who enjoys teaching clients about the valuation process.

Chapter 2 | *Valuation Fundamentals*

- Valuators should be willing to defend their work. I have testified at trials and depositions dozens of times, and it is not easy defending your work in stressful situations. Not all valuations end up in conflicts; however, it is good to know that your valuator will not fold under pressure if the IRS or anyone else questions the valuation.
- Ask for recommendations from professionals and other business owners. Bankers, CPAs, lawyers, and investment advisors are good professionals to ask.

Once you select a valuator and subsequently receive your report, ask yourself these questions when reviewing the valuation:

- Did the valuator really understand the business?
- Did the valuator consider the future industry trends and how the business will perform in different economic cycles?
- Did the valuator use widely recognized valuation methods?
- Does it appear that the valuation is a prophecy of the future?

A valuation report prepared by a member of one of the organizations listed previously is required to follow certain reporting standards. In order for you to understand what should be included in your valuation report and the definition of some the terms typical used in a valuation, I have included a summary of the valuation reporting requirements from the AICPA Statement on Standards for Valuation Services No. 1 and a glossary of valuation terms (see Appendix C).

Tip This final question needs to be asked after reviewing a business valuation: *Would you buy the business at the price that the valuator concluded?* If so, the valuation is probably realistic.

When Is a Valuation Needed?

Valuations are needed in a variety of situations. If someone dies and owns stock in a company, the IRS wants to know the value to determine any estate tax owed. If a business owner is going through a divorce, the husband and wife both need to know the value in order to correctly split up the assets.

In my practice, I categorize business valuations into two different camps. The first is the "have to" valuations, and the second is the "should" valuations. The former valuations are driven by a specific event (i.e., death and divorce). The latter are valuations not driven by an event, but based on the business owner's desire to know the value of the business. Business owners need to know the "real value" in order to develop succession and estate plans, take steps to increase value, and properly position the business for a sale. In another words, they want a valuation in order to treat their business like an investment.

"Have To" Valuations

The majority of my valuation practice, as well as with other valuation professionals, involves preparing "have to" valuations. In these cases, there is an event that drives the client to pick up the phone and call a valuation professional, such as the following:

- *Death of a shareholder*: When a business owner dies, there are various parties that need to know the value of the decedent's interest. If the business owner's estate is large enough, the IRS requires an estate tax return to be prepared and the estate must send it a valuation that meets the 59-60 standards. For smaller estates, the heirs, other shareholders, and probate court will want to know the value.

- *Gifts of closely held stock*: A popular exit strategy is to gift stock of a closely held business to the next generation. Again, 59-60 must be followed in order for the gift to be accepted by the IRS. If the valuation meets the IRS standards, there is a three-year time period in which the IRS can question the value. After that, the IRS cannot make adjustments. If the valuation does not follow 59-60, there is no statute of limitations and the IRS can come back 5, 10, or 20 years later and impose additional taxes and penalties on the gift.

- *Equity compensation valuations*: If a business provides an equity incentive plan to their employees (including stock options or stock bonuses), a business valuation needs to be prepared. These incentive awards are considered to be compensation to the employees and the compensation level reported to the IRS is determined by a business valuation.

- *Dispute related to valuations:* There are two types of disputes that business valuators typically get involved with: divorce and shareholder disputes. If a business interest is a marital asset, it has to be valued just like any other marital asset. It is rare when the business owner and the spouse just divide and each retain the stock in a company. Instead, once a value is determined, the business owner writes a check to the spouse for his portion of the business value and she keeps the company. Shareholder disputes are just as common as divorce valuations. If shareholders want to leave a business or are forced out, they need a valuation to determine the value of their ownership interest.

  As you can imagine, these valuations can be quite adversarial. Sometimes, the parties hire one valuation professional who acts like a mediator and the valuation issue is resolved quickly. Other times, the parties hire their own valuation expert and each side "dukes it out" in court. Then a judge with no business background decides what the company should be worth.

- *ESOPs:* An ESOP is a qualified retirement plan where the employees own the stock. A valuation is required when the ESOP is established and also is required on an annual basis. When the ESOP is established, a valuation is needed to determine the buy-out price paid to the shareholder selling to the ESOP. After that, there are annual ongoing valuations that set the price per share that gets allocated to the employees' individual accounts. When employees leave the company, their shares are bought out based on the annual valuation.

- *Other situations that require a business valuation:* This is not all inclusive, but these are other events that will require the business owner to obtain a business valuation: bankruptcy, converting from a C-Corporation to an S-Corporation, a charitable contribution of closely held stock, or an allocation of intangible assets after buying another business.

"Should" Valuations

Some valuations are not driven by a specific event but are important for the business owner to have. There is no court date, IRS deadline, or anything else that drives the business owner to pick up the phone and hire someone to prepare a business valuation.

These valuations are used by business owners to make important decisions about their future. We have discussed why this is important in the opening chapter of this book. The following are some specific reasons why business owners have hired us to prepare valuations that are not based on a specific event:

- Estate planning
- Succession planning
- Selecting the appropriate exit strategy
- Determining life insurance needs
- Looking for ways to increase the value of the business
- Setting a value in a buy-sell agreement
- Setting up incentive plans for management

There is another reason why we are hired for a valuation project that is in-between the "have to" and "should" valuations. This is for merger and acquisition (M&A) purposes. There is no requirement that you obtain a business valuation when someone wants to buy your business. But certainly it would be wise to have a professional assist you when you are thinking about selling your most valuable asset. The same goes for buying a business. You can pay what you want. But if you are going to make a major investment, it would be wise to have a trained set of eyes providing you with advice on how much you should pay.

Now that you have an understanding of the valuation profession and when a valuation is needed, it is time to talk about the valuation engagement.

The Valuation Engagement

I am amazed at how often business owners obtain a business valuation, and it does not deliver what they need. This is due to a misunderstanding at the beginning of the process. The business owner does not understand what is being valued and the standard of value being used. Any valuation engagement should be spelled out in the beginning of the process with an engagement letter. This step ensures that the valuator and the business owner are on the same page (see example in Appendix A). These are the four major areas that should be clarified in the engagement letter:

- What is being valued
- How the value is defined (standard of value)
- The date of the valuation
- The purpose of the valuation

What Is Being Valued?

The first question a valuator should ask a business owner is, "What are we valuing?" A common response from a business owner is this: "What do you mean by what are we valuing? Just tell me what my business is worth, so I can see if I can retire."

Unfortunately, many business owners are unpleasantly surprised at the level of proceeds they receive from the sale of their business. They expect a certain amount of dollars after the sale but can receive significantly less when the deal is done. How can this be?

This is due to two factors. The first is a lack of understanding of the difference between enterprise value and equity value. The second is that the seller did not factor in the impact of income taxes and transaction costs. This is very important to understand. To make sure this is clear to you, I have added examples at the end of this chapter.

Enterprise Value vs. Equity Value

Enterprise value is simply the value of the business operations. Sometimes it is called the operating value. Enterprise value includes the company's working capital, fixed assets, goodwill, and other intangible assets. It excludes the value of assets that are not needed to operate the business (nonoperating assets) and almost all liabilities except accounts payable and accrued expenses. For example, any long-term debt with a bank is excluded when determining the enterprise value. Enterprise value is typically the selling price for the business operations.

The equity value is the value of the stock of a company. It is determined by adding to the enterprise value any nonoperating assets and subtracting out the obligations of the company that are not typically assumed by the buyer of the business. Equity values are often calculated in the case of divorces and for estate planning purposes. Here is the formula for determining the equity value:

Equity Value = Enterprise Value + Nonoperating Assets − Liabilities Not Assumed

Nonoperating assets are items that are owned by the business that are not necessary for the day-to-day operations. Examples of nonoperating assets include vacation homes, luxury cars, excess cash, and life insurance cash surrender value.

Typically a buyer of a business will assume a limited amount of liabilities (accounts payables and accrued expenses). After the transaction, the seller pays off the other obligations of the company, including any bank debt.

The valuator and the client need to clarify what value is needed—the equity value or the enterprise value.

Net Proceeds from a Sale of a Business

In Chapter 5, we will discuss the difference between an asset sale and a stock sale. There is a huge difference between the two. Under an asset sale, the proceeds received from the sale are collected through the business entity and the business is liquidated. Then the remaining proceeds after paying off all retained debt and liabilities are distributed to the equity owners. In a stock sale, business owners simply sell their stock and walk away. This option is much simpler and better for the seller, but a stock sale rarely occurs. For now, we will focus on what happens with an asset sale.

Under an asset sale, the proceeds from selling the business's operating assets are paid to the business entity. The amount received is reduced by transaction costs and paying off all remaining liabilities. Transaction costs include fees paid to business brokers, lawyers, and accountants. Before business owners can spend or invest the proceeds from the sale, they have to factor in the tax consequences of the transaction. The amount of the total taxes owed depends on many factors and can be up to 50% of the selling price. Tax consequences on asset and stock deals will also be explained in more detail in Chapter 5.

Another issue that should be clarified at the start of the valuation process is what percentage of the business entity is being valued. Is it a 100% interest or something less than that? A minority interest is a stake in a company that is less than 50%. It is worth less on a per share basis than a controlling interest. This is due to the severe limitations that minority owners have. We will talk more about this in the next chapter.

How the Value Is Defined

There are a few different standards of values that are used in the valuation profession. Standard of value simply means how value is defined. It is very important that business owners understand which standard of value was used for their valuation conclusion. The valuation conclusion will not be the same for each standard of value. In this book, I will only focus on the "fair market value" and the "investment value" standard of value.

Fair market value is defined as the cash or cash equivalent price at which property would change hands between a willing buyer and a willing seller, neither being under a compulsion to buy or sell, and both having reasonable knowledge of relevant facts.

Investment value is defined as the potential value to a strategic buyer. A strategic buyer is one who can realize synergistic benefits through the combined purchasing power of the new entity and the elimination of duplicate functions or competitive factors. Investment value is typically higher than fair market value. Sometimes it is called synergistic value.

Fair market value assumes that the buyer of a business will step into your shoes and have the same opportunities and cash flow that you have. Investment value assumes that the buyer will be able to make significant changes that will positively impact future cash flow.

Fair market value is used for most of the "have to" valuations. The IRS and the court system want to know the value based on current operations and not what the value is to a larger company that can achieve synergies from the purchase of the business.

Investment value is used in situations where the business owner wants to sell the business for top dollar and is curious what a larger business that can eliminate jobs and has other synergies will pay for the business. In these cases, we attempt to determine what the synergies will be to the buyer and anticipate their future cash flow. Sometimes a buyer is just interested in the seller's intellectual property (patents, software developed, etc.) and is willing to pay large dollar amounts even though the seller has not been profitable, owing to the buyer's ability to better utilize these assets and increase their cash flow.

This is why it is important to know what standard of value is used in the valuation. Sometimes I will show the business owner the value under both the fair market value and the investment value standard. This is helpful in choosing what exit strategy makes the most sense. Some business owners want top dollar for their business and are willing to sell to a larger business, even though they know it means many jobs will be eliminated. Other business owners are willing to accept a lower selling price if they are assured that their employees will keep their jobs.

The Purpose of the Valuation

Earlier in this chapter, we discussed the reasons someone may need to have a valuation prepared. It is very important that the purpose of the valuation be clear in the beginning of the process since the standard of value used is based on the purpose of the valuation.

In addition, there are many times when someone will try to use a valuation done for one purpose for another purpose or the valuation prepared for one purpose gets used for another purpose. I hate it when I get calls from divorce attorneys saying that they have a copy of a valuation done for business planning purposes and they want to use it in a divorce case. Is the valuation conclusion the same? It depends on the standard of value used and the date of the valuation.

The Date of the Valuation

The valuation is always as of a specific date. The determination of the valuation date is very simple in the case of an estate (day of death) or gift (date of the gift) but can be much harder to determine in other cases. A divorce is an example of where the date can be confusing. Is it the date of separation? The date of the final court hearing? It is important that the date of the valuation is clearly established between the valuator and the client.

In valuation theory, events that occur after the date of the valuation should not be considered unless they are reasonably foreknown. One day can make a big difference in the valuation conclusion. A company with a devastating fire that was not properly insured is worth significantly less the day after the fire than it was the day before.

Now that you understand what needs to be clarified before starting a valuation engagement, let's discuss the relevant factors that should be considered during the valuation process.

Important Factors to Consider in a Valuation

Valuing a business is not a simple and quick process. There are many factors that need to be considered before coming to a conclusion on a company's value.

The following is an excerpt from IRS Revenue Ruling 59-60:

> It is advisable to emphasize that in the valuation of the stock of closely held corporations or the stock of corporations where market quotations are either lacking or too scarce to be recognized, all available financial data, as well as all relevant factors affecting the fair market value, should be considered.

What are the relevant factors? The following is not an all-inclusive list of the relevant factors, but these factors are fundamental and require careful analysis in each case:

- *An in-depth understanding of the business*: Valuation analysts need to know all they can about the business and its operations. This includes knowing the strength of the management team, the products and services sold, the customers, the suppliers, what keeps management awake at night, and what they are excited about. This is very important in determining how risky it is to buy the business and what "rate of return" the buyer requires in order to make an investment in the business.

- *Historical financial trends of the business*: During the past few years, has the business been growing or declining? Are the profit margins improving or deteriorating? Are the financial results consistent or unpredictable? Will these trends continue into the future?

- *Economic outlook where the business operates*: The revenue and profit of some companies are tied directly to the overall economy of where they operate (e.g., a construction-related company). The expected future operating results are tied directly to the forecast for the economy. Meanwhile, other companies are not impacted by how the overall economy is doing because they have developed products that sell in good and bad times (e.g., Apple).

- *Industry outlook*: Understanding the outlook of the specific industry where the business operates is critical in any valuation. For example, in the 1980s typewriting manufacturers may have had very good historical financial trends; however, the outlook for the industry was poor due to the acceptance of the personal computer and word processing software. Within a few years, there were no longer any manufacturers of typewriters.

- *Management's forecast of the future*: Valuation is a prophecy of the future. It is critical that the valuation analyst spend a great amount of time discussing with management their expectations for the future and understand any reasons why it may deviate from recent historical trends. The valuator needs to have a skeptical mind when dealing with management forecasts and make a judgment call whether to believe them or not. This is particularly true when management wants a certain outcome. For instance, is it a coincidence that owners talk about all the bad things happening to their business, and how the future will be much worse than the past, when they are going through a divorce?

Only after valuators believe that they have a good understanding of a business and its prospects for the future can they begin determining the value of a business.

The Three Valuation Approaches

In my profession, there are three recognized approaches in determining the value of a business. Under each approach, there are many different accepted methodologies in determining value. The three approaches to value are the income, asset, and market approach. In the next chapter, we will discuss these in more detail.

The Income Approach to Value

This is the most widely used and accepted approach in valuing a business. In the simplest terms, this approach determines the future economic benefit the buyer will obtain from buying the business and then determines the rate of return required to entice an investor to buy the business. This is similar to any other investment that you may consider investing in. Two questions need to be asked: what can I earn on the investment and how risky is that investment?

The Asset Approach to Value

This approach estimates the value of the tangible assets owned by the business (cash, receivables, inventory, and equipment) and the amount of the business's obligations (payables, payroll, taxes, and bank debt) as of the valuation date. The difference between the value of the assets and the obligations is the value under this approach. When this approach is higher than the other approaches, it means the business is worth more dead than alive and the valuator should factor in the cost to liquidate the assets into cash in determining the final value.

The Market Approach to Value

The most effective way to appraise your house is to find the sale price of other houses in your neighborhood that have recently sold. The market approach to value a business is similar to what real estate appraisers do. The valuator tries to find companies that are similar to the business being valued that have sold in the marketplace or are publicly traded. My firm subscribes to various databases that provide us with information about private company transactions. For some businesses, like a McDonald's restaurant, it is easy to find transactions and make the comparison to determine value. While for others, like a niche manufacturer, it is more difficult to find a comparable company and use the market approach.

We will discuss which approach makes the most sense in the valuation engagement in the next chapter. Many appraisers make the mistake of averaging the three approaches. This rarely is the best way to form a conclusion of value.

Valuation Definitions

At the end of the chapter, I present some very basic calculations that will enable you to understand the difference between enterprise value, equity value, and net proceeds. But first you need to understand two other concepts that will help you better understand these examples.

- *Sustainable cash flow*: This is the forecasted cash flow level that buyers expect to be able to put into their pocket on an annual basis. The sustainable cash flow is what is available after all expenses and taxes are paid and funds are retained for making investments into capital items (e.g., equipment). It is the cash produced by the business over and above what is needed to sustain operations. In other words, it is what the business owner can spend or invest.

- *EBITDA*: This popular financial acronym stands for "earnings before interest, taxes, depreciation, and amortization." It is how much cash is available before paying taxes and making investments into equipment, trucks, and other capital items. The term EBITDA is widely used in the valuation profession. A popular way to determine the enterprise value is taking the company's EBITDA level and multiplying it by an EBITDA multiplier, which changes depending on the industry, risk factors, and growth rate.

Valuation in Plain English

Armed with those two definitions, let's proceed. Remember that one of the most important concepts in valuation theory is that valuation is a prophecy of the future. Prophecy of what? It is the prophecy of the economic benefit available to the business owner. In other words, it is how much they pull out of the business on an annual basis and spend or invest.

When someone buys a business, there are two main questions that need to be answered before determining what price to pay for it:

- How much cash will I put into my pocket from buying this business? (This is the sustainable cash flow.)
- How sure am I that it will go into my pocket? (This is the required rate of return related to the sustainable cash flow.)

The buyer will perform, or hire someone to perform, a detailed analysis to answer these questions.

How Much Cash Will I Put into My Pocket?

The starting point in determining the sustainable cash flow is to normalize the historical financial statements. With this step, I make adjustments for unusual or nonrecurring items that would cause any particular year not to be truly representative of the operating results. For example, a one-time settlement payment from a lawsuit of $500,000 is not a recurring item and part of normal business operations. The next chapter will include more extensive information about the normalized process.

The normalized process provides us with historical financial trends that exclude items that are not part of the normal business operations. Does the historical normalized financial statement provide us with the best indication of the future? It might. It depends on what we learn from our study of the industry and our management interviews. For example, the historical trends are of no value to us if the business lost its largest customer, one that comprised 90% of sales.

Business owners cannot increase their lifestyle—send their kids to expensive colleges, add a vacation home, and so on—based on the normalized income level. Before business owners can put cash into their pocket, they need to consider the following:

- What will be Uncle Sam's cut of the profits?
- What big items need to be purchased to sustain operations?
- How much should be set aside to fund the growth of the business?

After paying taxes and setting aside funds to make major purchases and meet working capital needs, business owners can make cash distribution and do what they want with the funds.

How Sure Am I That It Will Go into My Pocket?

After the future sustainable cash flow is determined, it is important to determine the confidence level that a buyer would have in obtaining this cash flow. If buyers are very confident that it will land in their pocket, then they are willing to pay more for the business. If they are worried that the cash flow will not be there in three years, then they will not pay as much.

Valuators go through a process to determine what the proper rate of return should be for the business they are valuing, which includes looking at the specific risks associated with the business. This process will be explained more in the next chapter, and it is just as critical as determining the future sustainable cash flow. Small differences in this rate will make a significant difference in value.

The rate of return can only be determined by fully understanding the company's risk profile and prospects for future growth. This is done by studying the industry and interviewing management. It is critical that the valuator truly understands all the risks associated with the business being valued.

■ **The Key Valuation Concept in Plain English** How much can I put into my pocket by buying this business, and how sure am I that it will go into my pocket?

Besides knowing the answers to these two questions—how much and how certain—the answer to one additional question will determine the total price a buyer will pay for the business and the total proceeds the seller will obtain. This last question to ask is this: what am I buying? The business operations only, the enterprise value? Or the stock of the company, which includes the enterprise value?

Examples in Plain English

The best way to ensure that you fully understand the concepts presented in this chapter is by walking you through a simple example.

Scenario: Charlie is the 100% owner of a company that manufactures footballs, Fantastic Footballs, Inc., and he wants to sell his business. He has found a buyer and agreed to sell the business operations but not the stock of the company. The buyer and seller have agreed that the future sustainable EBITDA will be $800,000. They have agreed to use a multiplier of 5 of the estimated sustainable EBITDA to determine the enterprise value. The business owns a vacation home that is valued at $500,000, and it has a long-term bank debt of $2 million. The buyer does not want the vacation home and will not be paying off the debt at closing.

Enterprise Value Example

The enterprise value is the value of the company's operating assets (intangibles, fixed assets, and working capital). In this example, the buyer has agreed to pay 5 times EBTIDA for these operating assets. The enterprise value of the company is calculated here:

Sustainable EBITDA	$	800,000
Multiplier Applied		5.0
Enterprise Value	$	4,000,000

Since it is an asset deal, the company will obtain a check for $4 million at closing. After closing, the assets of Fantastic Footballs will be a cash of $4 million and a vacation home of $500,000. The only remaining obligation is the bank debt of $2 million. What is the value of the company's equity?

100% Equity Value Example

Charlie is excited that he sold his business for a good price and is comfortable about how the new owner will operate the business. He is anxious to invest the proceeds of the sale with his investment advisor. Since he sold only the operating assets of the business, the value of Charlie's equity is determined by adding back the nonoperating assets and subtracting the value of the liabilities that are not part of the enterprise value. The equity value of the business is calculated here:

Sustainable EBITDA	$ 800,000
Multiplier Applied	5.0
Enterprise Value	4,000,000
Vacation Home	500,000
Long-term Debt	(2,000,000)
100% Equity Value	$ 2,500,000

Charlie is surprised to learn that his equity value is not the 5 times EBITDA. In his retirement calculations, he assumed that he would have $4 million before taxes. He did not realize in the beginning of the selling process that the buyer would not be paying off his long-term debt. He needs to deduct the bank debt to determine how much he would realize after the sale and after he liquidates his company. But wait, there is one more surprise. Charlie must take one more step before he can spend or invest the money from the sale of his business.

Net Proceeds Example

Charlie's retirement plan is to travel the world and spoil his grandkids. He thought that $4 million was enough to do this. Charlie's stock is valued at $2.5 million after including the vacation home and the bank debt. Is this the amount that Charlie can give his investment advisor? No, it is not. Before he is able to spend or invest his sales proceeds, he must pay the tax man and the people that helped him sell his business.

Professional fees for a business transaction can include a success fee paid to an M&A intermediary or a business broker and fees paid to lawyers and accountants. In the following example, we will assume that the professional fees associated with selling Charlie's business totaled $250,000.

Of course, you would expect that Uncle Sam wants to get a piece of the action. There are tax consequences in selling a business. The taxes paid depend on whether it is an asset sale or a stock sale and how the transaction is characterized in the purchase agreement. We will assume that the total tax paid on this transaction was $750,000. Fantastic Footballs is a C-Corporation and the tax includes a corporate tax on the sale proceeds over and above the company's asset tax basis. In addition, Charlie must pay a tax on an individual basis after he liquidates the business to get his proceeds. We will explain the tax consequences of selling a business further in Chapter 5.

Charlie's net proceeds from this deal after paying the transaction costs and the IRS are calculated here:

100% Equity Value	$ 2,500,000
Income Taxes	(750,000)
Transaction Costs	(250,000)
Net Proceeds	$ 1,500,000

Charlie is not happy. He thought he was going to walk away with $4 million, but he instead is only getting $1.5 million!

Important It is critical that you know the difference between enterprise value, equity value, and net proceeds.

Summary

Hopefully after reading this chapter, you have a better understanding of the business valuation process. It is more complicated than simply putting numbers into a spreadsheet—but is less complicated than brain surgery.

As a business owner, it is vital that you understand the difference between enterprise value, equity value, and the net proceeds that you will receive after selling your business. Also it is important to know the difference between investment value and fair market value.

Now that you have a basic understanding on how a business is valued, let's move on to show more details about the valuation process. In the next chapter, we will explain further how your business is valued using the income, asset, and market approaches to value.

CHAPTER 3

Valuation Approaches
How the Sausage Is Made

Valuations for divorce cases and shareholder disputes are the closest we get to hand-to-hand combat in the accounting profession. Two valuation experts battle on the witness stand. We fight over future cash flows and what the expected rate of return should be on the cash flows. We have reams of paper to support our positions and hope that the attorney on our side asks the right questions and that the opposing attorney asks the wrong ones. However, many times none of this matters. The ultimate decision makers are the judges who probably neither have a business background nor enjoy listening to number nerds debate high-dollar issues. Sometimes their decisions are well thought out and make sense with the facts of the case. Other times, it is clear they did not really understand valuation theory, or they may have had an alternative motive with their decision. Going to trial on valuation issues is litigation roulette because it is hard to predict where the answer will land.

I have testified over two dozen times, including in front of a sleeping, snoring judge as well as before a plaintiff and defendant making obscene gestures at each other during my testimony. What follows are two real-life combat stories that will show you some difficulties in preparing a business valuation.

Hand-to-Hand Combat

The first case is called *"a tweak here and a tweak there make a big difference."* A few years ago, I was hired to provide two valuations of a manufacturing company for a domestic case. The owner started the business before he was married; therefore, I had to value the company at the date of the marriage and at the date of the divorce. The spouse was entitled to 50% of the growth in the value of the company between those two dates. In my opinion, the growth in value between the two dates was $2 million. At the last minute, the business owner's spouse hired a valuation expert, and he had very little time to produce a report. He decided to use my reports and just slightly change my cash flow assumption and my expected rate of return on the cash flow for both valuations. By only changing two assumptions, he concluded that the growth in value between the marriage and divorce date was $6 million—a huge difference created by only a couple of tweaks of my report. We provided testimony for over a week telling the judge why the other valuator was wrong and why our analysis was superior. Afterward, we shook hands and asked each other about our families since we were friends. The judge selected an amount that was in between our conclusions.

The second case, I call *"the 30-minute clock cleaning,"* shows the difficulty of using and supporting the market approach to value. I was hired by a divorce court to provide a valuation for both parties of a small retail store. No big deal, I thought. It turned out to be a very difficult case. The husband accused the wife of fraud, and it was difficult to obtain financial data. I felt that I could not rely on the income approach since the reported financial data was suspect. However, I was able to locate many transactions of similar type stores that could be used to determine the value of the company based on reported revenues and adding an amount for unreported cash. Since the court had hired me, I had expected to walk into court and give about an hour of testimony, have everyone be impressed with my wisdom, and then thank me as I walked out of the courtroom. The husband's attorney asked the court for a 30-minute recess to examine my file. When the recess was over, he proceeded to discredit my market method in the eyes of the judge. How could I compare a retail store located in a small city in Ohio to one that was located in Albany, New York or in Cleveland, Ohio? This went on for another 30 minutes. I attempted to explain why this approach was valid, but I have to admit that he did a great job of raising serious questions about the validity of the market data with only a 30-minute review of my file.

The point of telling you about these two cases is twofold. First of all, small changes in the assumptions will make a big difference in value. Second, I believe that the income approach is superior to the market approach since it is so difficult to find comparable companies that have sold that are similar to yours. As I explained in the previous chapter, there are only three recognized approaches in determining the value of a business. Under each approach, there are several different methods that can be deployed to determine value. Both the market approach and the asset approach have their places, but in the real world, the income approach is what is used to buy and sell businesses. Therefore, we will focus on the income approach in this chapter and provide limited insight on the market and asset approaches to value.

The Income Approach to Value

This approach values your business like any other investment. When using this approach, I pretend that I am buying the business and determine how much I am willing to pay for it. The amount I am willing to pay depends on my assumptions about the future cash flow and how much risk is related to that cash flow. The keys to this approach are answering the questions that were introduced in the last chapter:

- How much cash will I put into my pocket from buying this business? (This is the sustainable cash flow.)

- How sure am I that it will go into my pocket? (This is the required rate of return related to the sustainable cash flow.)

Once those questions are answered, the valuator is able to determine the enterprise value.

There are two primary methods that valuators use when applying the income approach. Sometimes both methods are used, but most of the time the valuator chooses between one of the two:

- *Single-stream capitalization method*: This method is used when the future cash flow is anticipated to be relatively stable and has a constant rate of long-term growth. The sustainable cash flow is determined and then reduced to a single unchangeable amount that is expected to continue indefinitely. The required rate of return using this method is called the capitalization rate (discount rate less a long-term sustainable growth rate). The sustainable cash flow is divided by the capitalization rate to determine the present value of the future cash flows, which is the enterprise value.

- *Discounted cash flow method*: This method is used when a company's future cash flows are not expected to be stable and cannot be reduced to a single number. This method projects the future revenues, profits, and cash flows over a number of years (projection period). Beyond a certain point of time, it is assumed that the company will continue to grow cash flow at a constant rate. A mathematical formula determines the "terminal value" of a company at the end of the projection period. This terminal value is the present value of the future cash flows after the projection period. The present value of the future cash flows from the projection period plus the terminal value equals the enterprise value.

Under each method, it is important to estimate the expected future revenues and cash flows based on fully understanding the business and its prospects for the future. This is done through financial, industry, and economic analysis and discussions with management. After performing this analysis, the valuator will decide whether to use the single-stream capitalization or discounted cash flow method. The method selected depends on whether the expected future cash flow can be reduced to a single amount. The following are situations when the discounted cash flow method is preferred over the single-stream capitalization method:

- The company's growth rate is expected to be very high, inconsistent, or negative.
- Management knows that future results will be variable due to known factors. This could include the loss of a major customer or the introduction of a new product line.
- The company will wind down operations due to a known event.

We will focus on the single-stream capitalization method in this chapter, which is much easier to understand and apply. This will allow you to understand the basic theory behind the income approach.

Let's now turn our attention to how the sustainable cash flow is determined.

How Much Cash Will I Put into My Pocket?

No matter what method is used, it is critical that the valuator understand the historical financial trends and be able to determine what the true historical earnings have been. Financial statements may not tell the real story. A business may appear to be unprofitable, but in reality is very profitable and vice versa.

Valuing and Selling Your Business

Business owners manage their bottom line to provide themselves with the highest after-tax proceeds (from the combination of wages and profits). Also, certain events happen to a business that impact the reported profit levels, but they may not be recurring or normal for the business operations. It is important that the valuator normalize the historical numbers in order to understand what the true historical earnings have been.

The Normalization Process

The starting point in determining the sustainable cash flow is to normalize the historical financial statements. The normalization process restates the financial statements to exclude items that are not part of the normal business operations.

The first step in the normalization process is to summarize the historical earnings levels. I like to use EBITDA (earnings before interest, taxes, depreciation, and amortization) in my analysis. I usually summarize at least five years of the historical EBITDA amounts and also add back owner's compensation. From this amount, I make adjustments to the historical earnings to normalize the earnings and make them comparable with others in the industry. The following are adjustments that are made to normalize historical earnings:

- Extraordinary or nonrecurring income and expense items
- Expenses that are not standard in the industry
- Owner's compensation that is either higher or lower than fair market wages
- Income or expense items relating to nonoperating assets

The best way for you to understand the normalization process is to go through a scenario. We will continue with the Fantastic Footballs, Inc. scenario that was presented in Chapter 2. The following chart summarizes Fantastic Footballs' five-year revenue and EBITDA trends:

	2008	2009	2010	2011	2012
Sales	$ 6,000,000	$ 5,000,000	$ 5,500,000	$ 6,000,000	$ 6,500,000
Sales Growth %	5.0%	-16.7%	10.0%	9.1%	8.3%
Income Before Taxes	300,000	-	(100,000)	300,000	400,000
Interest Expense	100,000	90,000	80,000	90,000	100,000
Depreciation and Amortization	100,000	100,000	100,000	100,000	100,000
EBITDA	$ 500,000	$ 190,000	$ 80,000	$ 490,000	$ 600,000

Chapter 3 | Valuation Approaches

The historical EBITDA has ranged from $80,000 to $600,000. Is this a true reflection of Fantastic Footballs' historical earnings?

Owner's compensation is an area where there is a great deal of discretion and differences between businesses. Business owners pay themselves differently depending on the business entity type (C-Corporation, S-Corporation, LLC, etc.), their financial needs, and the health of the business. They do not compensate themselves the same way they compensate their employees. Employees are paid based on their roles, skills, and value to the business. Properly normalizing owner's compensation is very important. Because of this, we add back owner's compensation in the analysis prior to making any normalization adjustments to isolate the owner's compensation issue. The following is the same analysis, but showing the historical EBITDA before owner's compensation (EBITDAOC):

	2008	2009	2010	2011	2012
Sales	$ 6,000,000	$ 5,000,000	$ 5,500,000	$ 6,000,000	$ 6,500,000
Sales Growth %	5.0%	-16.7%	10.0%	9.1%	8.3%
Income Before Taxes	300,000	-	(100,000)	300,000	400,000
Interest Expense	100,000	90,000	80,000	90,000	100,000
Depreciation and Amortization	100,000	100,000	100,000	100,000	100,000
EBITDA	500,000	190,000	80,000	490,000	600,000
Owner's Compensation	500,000	300,000	400,000	500,000	500,000
EBITDA and Owner's Compensation	$ 1,000,000	$ 490,000	$ 480,000	$ 990,000	$ 1,100,000

Once the EBITDAOC is determined, it is time to make the adjustments to normalize the EBITDA. Let's assume that Fantastic Footballs had a product liability suit in 2010. The cost to defend and settle the lawsuit was $250,000, and management indicated that lawsuits like this are rare. It was a one-time event that depressed the 2010 earnings, so we will add back to the EBITDA level the expenses related to this litigation. The next adjustment is for the way in which Fantastic Footballs records its inventory. The inventory is recorded by using a last-in, first-out (LIFO) method because it provides the company with a tax advantage. However, the first-in, first-out (FIFO) inventory method provides a truer picture of the actual value of the inventory and the cost of goods sold. Therefore, we will make an adjustment to convert the Fantastic Footballs' inventory from LIFO to FIFO.

The last adjustment is for owner's compensation. Charlie, the owner of Fantastic Footballs, is the CEO and receives a salary and a bonus based on the annual profits. To understand the true earnings capacity of Fantastic Footballs, we need to determine what Charlie's wages would be in the marketplace for the services he performs. This adjustment is made by understanding the number of hours that he works and services that he provides. Once we understand this, we examine various salary surveys to determine what it would cost to replace Charlie at fair market wages. The following is the normalized EBITDA calculation after making the previously mentioned adjustments:

	2008	2009	2010	2011	2012
Sales	$ 6,000,000	$ 5,000,000	$ 5,500,000	$ 6,000,000	$ 6,500,000
Sales Growth %	5.0%	-16.7%	10.0%	9.1%	8.3%
Income Before Taxes	300,000	-	(100,000)	300,000	400,000
Interest Expense	100,000	90,000	80,000	90,000	100,000
Depreciation and Amortization	100,000	100,000	100,000	100,000	100,000
EBITDA	500,000	190,000	80,000	490,000	600,000
Owner's Compensation	500,000	300,000	400,000	500,000	500,000
EBITDA and Owner's Compensation	1,000,000	490,000	480,000	990,000	1,100,000
Adjustments to Normalize EBITDA:					
Lawsuit Expense	-	-	250,000	-	-
Conversion to FIFO Inventory	50,000	(40,000)	70,000	60,000	50,000
Normalized Owner's Compensation	(300,000)	(300,000)	(300,000)	(300,000)	(300,000)
Normalized EBITDA	$ 750,000	$ 150,000	$ 500,000	$ 750,000	$ 850,000
Percentage of Sales	12.5%	3.0%	9.1%	12.5%	13.1%

You can see that there is quite a difference between the historical EBITDA and the normalized EBITDA levels. In 2010, the reported EBITDA was $80,000 and the normalized EBITDA was $500,000. That is a big difference! This is mainly due to the lawsuit expense and LIFO inventory depressing the net income and the fact that Charlie's compensation was higher than the fair market wages.

Important It is critical that you normalize the historical earnings. You will not be able to determine the future sustainable cash flows without preparing this analysis.

Determining the Sustainable Cash Flow

Now that the historical EBITDA has been normalized, we can begin the process of determining what the sustainable cash flow level should be for Fantastic Footballs. This is a two-step process. For the single-stream capitalization method, we must decide on a single amount that will represent Fantastic Footballs' future sustainable EBITDA. It is important that a great deal of effort is placed in determining this amount since a bad assumption will lead to a wrong valuation conclusion.

The normalized EBITDA has ranged between $150,000 and $850,000 during the past five years. The five-year average is $600,000. After hitting a low in 2009, the normalized EBITDA has increased each year. What EBITDA amount should we use? The latest year results of $850,000? The five-year average of $600,000? As you will see later in this chapter, there will be a big difference in the enterprise value depending on which EBITDA level is chosen.

The EBITDA level to use is dependent on understanding the historical trends, industry forecasts, and management's plausible forecast of the future. Perhaps the recent history will continue because Fantastic Footballs recently obtained a few new large customers. Maybe industry studies have shown that football has gained in popularity and that the future is bright for football manufacturers. If our analysis led us to believe that the positive trends would continue, then our chosen sustainable EBITDA level would be based on recent history.

Alternatively, we might have learned that the football industry is cyclical and that every five years Fantastic Footballs has some good years and some bad years. Management may have told us that they do not believe that the positive trends that started in 2010 will continue into the future. If this is true, then we may choose the five-year average of $600,000 as our sustainable EBITDA level.

Once we decide on the sustainable EBITDA level, we need to determine the sustainable cash flow. Business owners cannot put the EBITDA amounts into their pockets. Before this can happen, they must do the following:

- Pay income taxes.
- Buy new equipment to sustain operations.
- Be able to fund their working capital needs.

Let's continue on with our scenario. Let's assume that we selected $800,000 as the sustainable EBITDA level. This is because management believes that the most recent trends will continue for the foreseeable future. The bad results in 2009 were impacted by the recession and the issue surrounding the lawsuit. Management believes that future results will be slightly lower than the 2012 levels due to pricing pressures from the competition. After much analysis and discussion with management, we have decided that the sustainable EBITDA level is $800,000.

In order to convert the EBITDA level to cash, we must take account of income taxes, make an allowance for future capital expenditures, and determine future working capital needs. You have to pay taxes on your profits. You also have to make capital improvements (equipment, machinery, and building improvements) and have cash available to fund your growth (working capital needs) to sustain operations. The amount needed for working capital is a function of expected growth rate and the current working capital level.

In order to convert the sustainable EBITDA level to a sustainable cash flow level for Fantastic Footballs, we made the following adjustments:

- The taxable income is equal to the EBIT (earnings before interest and taxes). For this scenario, there is no interest expense. The taxable income is EBITDA less depreciation. The corporate income tax amount is based on a tax analysis.

- We have assumed that the future capital expenditure will average $100,000 a year. This is the amount needed to buy new equipment and make building improvements on an annual basis.

- The amount of cash that is needed to be retained to fund the growth in inventory and accounts receivable is $20,000.

The calculated sustainable cash flow is as follows:

Normalized EBITDA	$ 800,000
Depreciation Expense	(100,000)
Net Income Before Taxes	700,000
Corporate Income Taxes	(230,000)
Normalized Earnings After Taxes	470,000
Add Back: Depreciation	100,000
(Less): Capital Expenditures	(100,000)
(Less): Working Capital Needs	(20,000)
Future Sustainable Net Cash Flow	$ 450,000

Based on this analysis, the buyer of Fantastic Footballs can expect to put $450,000 on an annual basis in his pockets. This assumes that the buyer pays fair market wages for CEO services and that there are no unusual or nonrecurring items. In other words, the $450,000 is the amount that he can do with as he wants since there is no need to retain this amount in the business. How much are investors willing to pay for a $450,000 cash flow stream? It depends on how confident they are that the $450,000 will go into their pocket.

How Sure Am I That It Will Go into My Pocket?

Now that the sustainable cash flow has been determined, it is time to develop the appropriate rate of return needed to entice a buyer to invest in Fantastic Footballs. This rate is developed by understanding Fantastic Footballs' individual risk profile and its prospects for future growth. In addition, it is important for the valuator to have a basic understanding of investment theory and the rate of returns available on alternative investments.

Chapter 3 | Valuation Approaches

There are two important concepts behind the development of the required rate of return. The first is risk, and the second is the time value of money. We have previously mentioned the direct relationship between risk and the rate of return. The higher the risk associated with an investment, the higher the rate of return that is required to entice an investor. The concept of time value of money is that a dollar now is worth more than a dollar received in the future. The value of a company is the present value of the future cash flows. You must account for both risk and the time value of money when valuing a company.

There are three important terms that valuators use when determining the rate of return required by the investor in a business:

- *Discount rate*: This is the rate required by investors to entice them to invest in a particular business. It is also called the cost of equity. The discount rate incorporates both the time value of money and the risk related to the company.

- *Capitalization rate*: This is the discount rate less the long-term growth rate of the company's cash flows.

- *Weighted average cost of capital (WACC)*: This is a company's capital structure consisting of equity (investors) and debt (creditors). The enterprise value is determined based on the cash flow that is available to both equity owners and creditors. Therefore, the rate of return that is applied to the future cash flows is a blend of cost of the equity and debt.

Determining the Required Rate of Return

The first step in developing the rate of return is to determine the discount rate. This is the rate of return that an equity investor needs in order to invest in your business. There are two popular ways that valuation professionals use in determining the discount rate: the "build-up" approach and the capital asset pricing model (CAPM). The build-up approach is based on the premise that a company's discount rate is composed of a number of identifiable return factors that are added together, or "built up," into a total required rate of return. CAPM theory holds that the cost of equity is equal to the risk-free rate of return, plus a risk analysis based on similar companies that are publicly traded. The major difference between the two approaches is that the CAPM adds an analysis of public market data to the discount rate calculation. Each approach includes a risk premium component that reflects the fact that investors must be paid to take any risk above that of a "risk-free" investment. The difference between the risk-free rate of return and the total return from an equity investment is called a *risk premium*.

The rest of this section will be devoted to the build-up approach in developing a discount rate. The CAPM is too complex for the purposes of this book and usually is applied in the valuation of very large companies.

The build-up approach follows this step-by-step process:

1. First, we determine what a risk-free investment is. In the valuation profession, long-term US Treasury bonds are considered to be risk-free investments. I prefer to use the 20-year US Treasury bond rate, as of the valuation date, for my risk-free rate.

2. The next step is to add an "equity risk premium." This is the premium that equity investors received in the US public markets over and above the risk-free return. We use the *Duff & Phelps LLC Risk Premium Report* to determine this equity risk premium. Recently, the equity risk premium has been in the 8% to 14% range. The level of the premium depends on the size of the business being valued. For companies with revenues of less than $100 million, the equity risk premium is at the high end of the range.

3. After applying an equity risk premium, we must decide whether to make an adjustment for industry risks. The risk profile for each industry is different, and the industry may be more risky or less risky than the general equity market. The Duff & *Phelps LLC Risk Premium Report* also provides industry risk profiles.

4. The final risk adjustment is called the specific company risk premium. This premium is determined by the individual characteristics of each business. Some businesses have large risk premiums while others have none or small premiums. This is one of the most subjective adjustments that valuators make and where most valuation battles are fought in conflict valuations. Some of the most popular adjustments are made for the following:

    - Customer concentration issues
    - Thin or inexperienced management team
    - Reliance on one or two key employees
    - Pending lawsuits
    - Violation of governmental regulations
    - Inconsistency of historical earnings

Chapter 3 | Valuation Approaches

- Competitive factors
- Limited access to raw materials and employees
- Life cycle of products or services

Let's return to the Fantastic Footballs scenario. The risk-free rate is based on the 20-year US Treasury Bond rate as of the valuation date. The equity risk and industry risk premium are based on the *Duff & Phelps LLC Risk Premium Report*. The final step is to determine the specific company risk premium. This is solely based on the valuator's subjective analysis. For Fantastic Footballs, it is a concern that one customer accounts for 25% of the total revenues. Also, the business is dependent on Charlie's relationships with his customers and the fact that he has not developed a sales force or a second line of executives. If something happened to Charlie, the customers may go elsewhere. The following is an example of determining the discount rate by using the build-up approach:

Long-term 20 Year US Treasury Bond Rate	3.0%
Equity Risk Premium	13.0%
Industry Risk Premium	1.0%
Specific Company Risk Premium	7.0%
Discount Rate	24.0%

Once a discount rate is developed, it is important to compare it with the returns of alternative investments. The source I like best for this step is the "Pepperdine Private Capital Markets Project—Survey Report 2014."[1] This survey provides the required rate of returns required by angel, venture capital, private equity and mezzanine investors. I make a comparison of my developed discount rate to the required returns of mezzanine investors and private equity groups (PEGs). Mezzanine investors provide debt (and sometimes equity) financing to businesses. The debt is usually not fully secured and is subordinate to other creditors. Per the Pepperdine survey, the typical return required by a mezzanine investor (up to $10 million investment) is in the 14% to 21% range and for PEGs (up to $10 million) is in the 23% to 28% range. This survey is an excellent gauge to use as a reasonableness test of the calculated discount rate. The rate of return required for very risky investments in a business could exceed 30%.

The WACC is based on the business's optimal capital structure. This is done by analyzing the debt structures of other companies in the industry and the company's debt capacity. To calculate the WACC, we multiply the returns

---

[1] Pepperdine University, "Pepperdine Private Capital Markets Project—Survey Report 2014," http://bschool.pepperdine.edu/appliedresearch/research/pcmsurvey/. This survey is free to anyone who requests it.

required for each component of capital (equity and debt) by its contribution to the total capital. The debt component is the cost of debt financing for the company on an after-tax basis. This is determined by using the company's current market interest rate for debt financing and reducing that rate for the tax benefit of paying interest. For Fantastic Footballs, let's assume that optimal capital structure is 70% equity and 30% debt and the market interest rate for its debt financing is 6.0% with an income tax rate of 33.0%. The required equity return is 24% as developed previously and the after-tax return of debt financing is 4%. Therefore, the WACC would be calculated this way:

	Rate	Weight Applied	WACC
Equity Factor	24.0%	70.0%	16.8%
Debt Factor	4.0%	30.0%	1.2%
Weighted Average Cost of Capital			18.0%

The calculation of the capitalization rate is a very simple calculation. It is the WACC less the long-term growth rate for the business. When I say long-term, I mean forever. One of the biggest mistakes that I see in other valuation reports is that the long-term growth rate is too high. I have been able to discredit another valuator by showing the court that the business being valued will be larger than Microsoft in 30 years based on the other valuator's growth rate. The growth rate should not be significantly higher than the overall growth rate for the industry and the U.S economy. It rarely is above 4.0%. If a business expects very high growth for the next few years, the discounted cash flow method should be used.

For Fantastic Footballs, we will use a 3.0% long-term growth rate and thus, the capitalization rate is 15.0% (WACC of 18% less the 3.0% growth rate).

Calculating the Enterprise Value

In the last chapter, I mentioned that the enterprise value is the price that you can sell your business operations for. To calculate the enterprise value of Fantastic Footballs by using the income approach, we simply divide the future sustainable cash flow by the developed required rate of return. The following is the enterprise value of the company by using the assumptions developed in this chapter:

Future Sustainable Net Cash Flow	$ 450,000
Required Rate of Return	15.0%
Enterprise Value	$ 3,000,000

Remember the case in the beginning of this chapter—*a tweak here and a tweak there makes a big difference?* Let's make a tweak here and there and see if this is true. Let's assume that another valuator prepared a valuation of Fantastic Footballs. He disagrees with me on only two assumptions. First, he believes that the future sustainable EBITDA should be the five-year average of $600,000 and that the sustainable cash flow is $300,000. Second, he disagrees with the 15.0% required return that I developed and believes it should be 20%. These changes do not seem large, but they make a significant difference in value as shown here:

Future Sustainable Net Cash Flow	$	300,000
Required Rate of Return		20.0%
Enterprise Value	$	1,500,000

Only two changes were made in the assumptions, but they made a huge difference. The changes don't appear to be major, but the valuation under the second example is one half of the original example. You can see why there are valuation battles in the courtroom and with the IRS. Who is right? We may never know since Fantasy Footballs, Inc. is not for sale.

The development of the sustainable cash flows and the required rate of return require many judgment calls by the valuator. Little changes mean big differences in value. This is why it is important for you to understand and be involved in the valuation process. Just as the income approach requires many subjective factors, so does the market approach.

The Market Approach to Value

You may be familiar with the market approach to value. Most of you have bought a house or have refinanced your mortgage. As part of the process, the bank requires an appraisal of your home. Appraisers locate homes in your neighborhood that have recently sold. They then compare the homes that have sold that are similar in size and location to your home. They may make some adjustments for square footage, a finished basement, and other items to the homes that have sold. With this data, appraisers make an estimate of the value of your home.

This is very effective. What better evidence of value than recent actual transactions of a similar type of investment?

Valuators attempt to do a similar process in valuing a business under the market approach. There is a search for similar types of companies (guideline companies) that have actually been sold or are publically traded. They make adjustments to the data obtained from the guideline companies. They then apply this information to the business being valued to determine a value under the market approach. However, meaningful and ample data from similar companies is a challenge to obtain. Many times, it is difficult to make the right conclusion. For this reason, I usually place less reliance on the market approach and use it to support the valuation conclusion arrived from the income approach.

The following are the two valuation methods that are used under the market approach when valuing a company:

- The Guideline Public Company Method
- The Guideline Transaction (Merger and Acquisition) Method

The Guideline Public Company Method uses the market data and share prices of publicly traded companies to derive a value. Valuators look for companies that are publicly traded and similar to the business being valued to serve as a benchmark in the valuation. Typically, I only use this method for companies with revenues in excess of $50 million. An exception is when I am valuing a community bank. There are hundreds of small community banks that are publicly traded.

This method is misapplied frequently. I have seen a valuation analyst try to use this method to value a small software company with $5 million in sales. The comparable companies used included Microsoft and Oracle, which is ridiculous. The only thing that Microsoft and a small software company have in common is that they develop and sell software. This is like comparing an NFL team to a middle school flag football team. They both play football, but that is all they have in common.

If guideline companies are located, the value of a company is based on multiples derived from publicly traded companies and ongoing earnings (e.g., net income and EBITDA).

The Guideline Transaction Method locates companies that have sold in the marketplace as a benchmark in valuing a company. Several databases are available that provide the actual sale transactions of closely held companies. These databases are populated by business brokers who self-report their transactions. For a business like McDonald's, this method can be used with confidence. Each McDonald's operates in a similar fashion, and there are a lot of transactions data to analyze. What about a football manufacturer? How about your business? How many businesses are like yours for which transaction data can be reviewed?

How do valuators prepare a market approach to value if they cannot find comparable companies or the data received is not reliable? What I do is use generic surveys (like the Pepperdine study) and other sources that provide transactional data by broad industries and size of business. The Pepperdine study provides the average EBITDA multipliers for different industries by size of business. This information comes from investment bankers and business brokers, and it is helpful in determining the reasonableness of the income approach conclusion.

In Chapter 2, we prepared a value of the enterprise value of Fantastic Footballs based on the market approach. Here is that calculation again:

Sustainable EBITDA	$ 800,000
Multiplier Applied	5.0
Enterprise Value	$ 4,000,000

There is one more approach that is used to value a business—the asset approach.

The Asset Approach to Value

This approach is effective for an asset holding company (real estate and liquid investments) and for companies that are worth more dead than alive. These companies have a significant amount of physical assets (inventory, equipment, and receivables) but minimal or no profits.

If the value under the asset approach is higher than the values calculated under the income approach and market approach, then the valuator should consider the value under an orderly liquidation. The liquidation method assumes that a company is worth more under a liquidation premise than a going-concern entity.

The asset approach values the individual assets and liabilities of the business. Under this approach, the fair market value of the assets less the company's total obligations is the value of the company.

This approach is usually not used in the valuation of a going concern. A company's value is determined by its ability to generate cash flow, not by the value of its assets individually. It generally carries little or no weight in comparison to the income and market approaches; therefore, we will not provide any further analysis on this approach.

Determining Equity Value

The equity value is another name for the value of the company's stock. This is what is valued and reported to the IRS when you make a gift to a child and the value that is used to divide assets in a divorce. As stated in Chapter 2, the equity value is determined by adding to the enterprise value the value of the nonoperating assets and subtracting out the obligations that are not typically assumed by a buyer of the business. Here is the formula of the equity value again:

Equity Value = Enterprise Value + Nonoperating Assets – Liabilities Not Assumed

The first step in determining the equity value is concluding what the enterprise value is. For Fantastic Footballs, Inc., we have prepared a value based on the income approach and the market approach. Let's assume under the asset approach that the value of Fantasy Footballs is $1.5 million. The following is a summary of the calculated values:

Enterprise Value	
Income Approach	$ 3,000,000
Market Approach	$ 4,000,000
Asset Approach	$ 1,500,000

What should our enterprise value conclusion be? Is it a simple average of the three approaches? Absolutely not! The asset approach should not be a factor for Fantastic Footballs since it is a going concern that has a nice profit level. Should the market approach be considered? It depends on how confident valuators feel about the comparable companies. Typically, more weight is placed on the income approach, and in this case we will conclude an enterprise value of $3.2 million.

Let's assume during our financial analysis that we discovered that Fantastic Footballs owns a large life insurance policy on Charlie. It has a death benefit of $5 million and a cash surrender value of $500,000. Tomorrow, the company could cash in the policy to the insurance company and receive $500,000. Even though the insurance policy is important, it is not necessary to operate the business. Nonoperating assets are items that are owned by the business that are not necessary for the day-to-day operations.

We will assume that Fantasy Footballs has a normal working capital level and a long-term bank note of $1.2 million. This note is a liability that would not be assumed in a typical business transaction and needs to be deducted to determine the equity value.

The following is the equity value of Fantasy Footballs with the previously mentioned assumptions:

Enterprise Value	$ 3,200,000
Cash Surrender Value Life Insurance	500,000
(Less): Interest Bearing Debt	(1,200,000)
Equity Value	$ 2,500,000

Value per Share

Our valuation conclusion usually includes a value-per-share amount. This should be a simple calculation, right? Take the equity value divided by the number of shares outstanding. Many times it is this simple, but other times it is not. If the business has stock options or other synthetic equity, additional calculations need to be made to determine the value per share.

There is a difference in the value per share between a controlling interest and one that does not have control. Why? If you own one out of 100 shares in a company, what can you do with that? Can you set your salary, declare a dividend, or force a sale of the company? The answers are no, no, and no. Only a majority shareholder can do those things. What rights does a minority shareholder have? It depends on your state and the language of your shareholder agreement (if you have one).

Because of the limitations associated with a minority interest, discounts are applied when valuators are asked to value a minority interest. The exception is if there is an agreement that says valuators should not apply the discounts in the valuation.

There are two discounts that valuators apply to a minority interest. The first is a lack of control discount (or minority interest discount), and the second is a marketability discount.

Valuators are often asked to prepare the valuation of a minority interest. Most requests are related to the gift of a company's stock from a parent to a child. The other situation is the exit of a shareholder from a business. This exit could be by choice or by force. Should a discount be applied in this situation? At times, there is disagreement among shareholders about whether these discounts apply. If you are a shareholder who has a minority interest, make sure that you have a buy-sell or shareholder agreement that specifies whether your interest should be reduced by the lack of control and a marketability discount.

There are many studies and court cases that can be examined to determine the appropriate discount level for a minority interest. I will not bore you with these studies or court cases. It is important for you know that the value per share for a minority interest is lower than the value per share for a controlling interest. Included next is the value-per-share calculation for Fantastic Footballs. Let's assume that there are 100 common shares outstanding and that the appropriate discount for the lack of control discount is 12% and the lack of marketability discount is 25%. The value of a minority nonmarketable common share is calculated as follows:

Controlling Interest Per Share	$ 25,000
Lack of Control (Minority) Discount	(3,000)
Marketable Minority Interest	$ 22,000
Lack of Marketability Discount	(5,500)
Nonmarketable Minority Interest	$ 16,500

The value of minority shareholder's' share of stock is 34% less than the value of a controlling interest. In the real world of valuation, a minority interest usually has a 20% to 50% reduction in value when compared with a controlling interest. The level of the discount depends on the company's dividend policy, written shareholder agreements, and whether there will be a liquidating event in the future (sale, public offering, or liquidation).

Summary

After reading this and the previous chapters, I hope you have a better understanding of the entire valuation process. It is not a very clean process, but it's not as messy as making sausage.

So if you call me and ask for a formula to value your business or ask for something quick and dirty, you will understand why I will say that I am not interested in assisting you. Valuation is so much more than a formula or putting numbers in a spreadsheet. The valuator has to really understand the business in order to develop the sustainable cash flow and to develop the appropriate rate of return.

Most valuators rely heavily on the income approach to value. This approach is the same mindset that someone buying your business will have. The market approach may apply to your situation depending on whether the valuator can locate comparable companies that have sold or are publicly traded. The asset approach is rarely used for a going concern. The exception is when the business owner can achieve more proceeds by liquidating the business than through continued operations.

Now that you have a good understanding of the entire valuation process, it is time to discuss ways to make your business more valuable. In the next chapter, we will discuss the various strategies you can implement to grow the value of your business.

CHAPTER 4

Growing Your Value

Becoming More Attractive

Tim is a single young man in his early 20s. He wants to get married, have three kids, and a house in the country with a couple of dogs. It's a great plan, but the only thing missing is a wife. At this point, Tim doesn't have a girlfriend or any prospects. Tim asked a couple of his good friends about the best way to find a girlfriend that could become his spouse. Should he use an online dating service? Can they introduce him to someone?

Will, Tim's best friend from childhood, calls him up and says that they need to talk. Will and Tim meet up at the local pub, and Will orders a couple of stiff drinks. He looks very uncomfortable and tells Tim that he has something very personal to tell him. He says, "My friend, before you start looking for a spouse you need to make yourself more attractive. You dress like a slob and don't brush your teeth or shower. You live in your parent's basement and drive a rusted-out car without a heater or air conditioner. You don't have a job or any prospects for a good job. And finally, when you meet a girl you only talk about yourself while looking at your shoes."

After what seems like an eternity to Will, Tim responds and says, "Thank you for telling me this. It took a great deal of courage to say these things to me, and I know you said it because you care about me." Will is now more at ease, and they continue their discussion. At some point, Tim says that over the next couple of years, he is not going to look for a girlfriend but instead concentrate on making himself a better "catch." They devise a plan that starts with Tim brushing his teeth and taking a shower.

You know by now that this is not a book about dating and personal improvement. The point of this story is that before you go out and look for a possible suitor for your business, you need to make it as attractive as possible. Even if you don't intend to sell your business soon, it is important that you consider ways to make your business more attractive and healthy. By doing so, you will more enjoyment in running your business, make more money, and make it easier to sell your business when you are ready to cash in.

Having the Mindset to Increase the Business Value

It all starts with a "mindset." Do you treat your business "like an investment" or as a vehicle to support your lifestyle? Business owners who have written goals and plans to increase their value will be more successful in increasing the value of their business than those who simply hope the value will increase without having any concrete plans on how to make that happen.

Once you understand what your business is worth, the next step is to set goals on where you want the value to be in the future. How much do you want your business to increase in value one year from now? Where do you want the value to be when you sell the business? Not many business owners take the time to set specific goals for their business value as well as written strategies to achieve those goals. The few that I've witnessed doing this have been much more successful in growing the value of their business than the typical business owner.

Important   You should include your valuation goals and the strategies to achieve these goals as part of your strategic plan and succession plan.

If you have no intention of selling your business, should you set goals and develop plans to increase its value? Absolutely! Setting a course to increase your business value today will provide you with many important benefits

Valuing and Selling Your Business

besides a higher selling price. The following are three key areas to focus on to increase your business value (Figure 4-1):

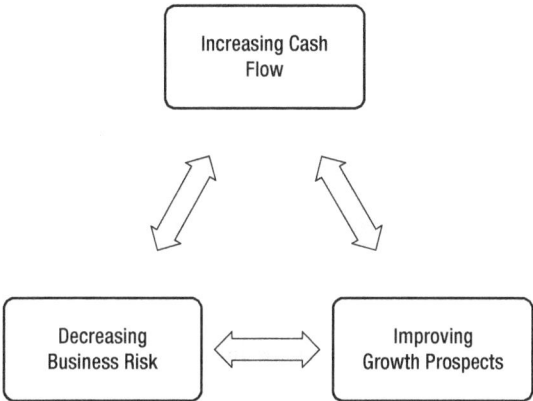

Figure 4-1. Focus on these three areas to increase your business value

How would you feel about your business if it had a better cash flow, fewer risks, and a higher growth rate? I bet it would be much easier to get out of bed in the mornings. If you can accomplish these three items, there will be a number of benefits besides a higher selling price:

- More cash available to distribute to yourself or to reinvest in your business
- Sleeping better at night with less stress and worry after reducing business risk
- A healthier business that will allow you to withstand a downturn in your industry or the economy
- Being able to react quickly to an selling opportunity that may present itself
- A more exciting and pleasant work atmosphere
- Increasing your retirement contributions, which will allow you to have greater flexibility in choosing your exit strategy

There are additional benefits as well, but it all starts with your decision to increase the value of your business and develop a plan to make your business more attractive to others.

If your business is the Brad Pitt or Angelina Jolie of the business world, you will have no problems obtaining suitors. You can skip the rest of this chapter. If not, please read on to learn about strategies to make your business more attractive. Besides increasing your cash flow, reducing your business risks, and developing a growth plan, it is important that your business does not have any hygiene issues that will turn off any potential buyers. Also, your business will be more attractive to suitors if it has a professional and sophisticated look to it. The remainder of this chapter is focused on making your business more valuable and attractive through the following strategies:

- Improving your business hygiene
- Increasing your sustainable cash flow
- Reducing your business risks
- Developing a growth plan
- Professionalizing your business

The best way to understand how these areas will impact your business value is to walk through a scenario. We will see how the value of Drew's business, Sensational Snacks, Inc., grows as we implement these strategies. You will be amazed by how much Drew's business increases in value without a major overhaul of the business.

Drew's Sensational Snacks

Drew is the 100% owner of Sensational Snacks, Inc., which is a manufacturer of potato chips and pretzels. The business has been in operation for 25 years, and Drew is the 60-year-old founder. He has a son and a daughter in the business and has not fully developed his exit strategy and succession plan. He wants to pass down the business to his kids, but he does not have enough money saved up to retire in the near future. Drew works 60 hours a week and is a control freak. He is the CEO and not a very good delegator. His daughter is in charge of accounting, and his son leads the purchasing department. The other members of the management team include the plant manager who has been with the business for 20 years and a sales manager who has worked for the company for 6 years. The following are some additional facts about the business:

- The business has one large customer: a supermarket chain that comprises 30% of revenues. The next two biggest customers account for 12% and 8% of revenues, respectively. Drew's top three customers are 50% of the total revenues.

- The historical sales and profit levels have been inconsistent. In the past five years, Drew had one great year, two decent years, and two bad years. His profits depend on potato prices, competitors' pricing actions, and the top three customers' buying habits.

Valuing and Selling Your Business

- The average annual growth rate has been 2% over the past five years. The industry forecasts 3.5% growth over the next five years.

- Drew takes out $220,000 a year in wages and has full benefits. In addition, the business pays for all of his family vehicle expenses and an annual "business trip" for the family. These additional benefits are in the $30,000 range annually.

- Drew is unsure about his exit strategy. He would like to see the business continue in the family, but he cannot afford to gift it to his children and they don't have the resources to buy it. Also, he can't decide which child would be the best leader.

- Outside of the business, Drew has a net worth of $1.2 million, with $700,000 in liquid investments (savings, stocks, bonds, and mutual funds) and $500,000 in real estate. His investment advisor has told him that he needs $3 million in liquid investments to retire at the lifestyle he wants at age 65.

Here is a summary of last year's income statement. These results are very similar to the average of the past five years. Some years have been better, and some have been worse. Drew believes that his results over the next few years will be similar.

Revenues	$ 6,000,000	100.0%
Cost of Goods Sold	4,200,000	70.0%
Gross Margin	1,800,000	30.0%
Operating Expenses	1,300,000	21.7%
Net Income Before Taxes	500,000	8.3%
Income Taxes	175,000	2.9%
Net Income	$ 325,000	5.4%

Based on these facts, what is Sensational Snacks' enterprise value on a fair market basis? Can Drew sell his business and have a comfortable retirement? Remember, "fair market value" basis does not factor in any synergistic benefits. For this example, let's assume that the sustainable cash flow is similar to the after-tax net income level. Based on this fact pattern, a buyer of Sensational Snacks can expect to put $325,000 in his pockets on an annual basis.

What is the required to entice someone to make an investment in Sensational Snacks? The risk concerns that a buyer would have include the following:

- The top three customers make up 50% of the revenues and the largest customer is 30% of revenues. The loss of the largest customer would be devastating.

Chapter 4 | Growing Your Value

- The business is very dependent on Drew. If something happened to him, business operations would suffer. There is no succession plan in place, and no one is specified to be the leader after Drew leaves. Outside of his son and daughter, there are only two individuals who are part of the management team.

- The historical earnings have been inconsistent. This is due to the volatility of potato prices and the fact that, at times, large competitors deeply discount their prices, hurting Drew's sales.

Based on these three major risk factors, it is determined that a 25% rate of return is required to entice an investor. The following is the calculated enterprise value:

Sustainable Net Cash Flow	$	325,000
Required Rate of Return		25.0%
Enterprise Value	$	1,300,000

At this point in time, Drew could sell the business operations for $1.3 million For the purpose of this example, let's assume that Sensational Snacks does not have any nonoperating assets or any liabilities that Drew will have to pay off when the business is sold. Therefore, the equity value equals the enterprise value. Let's also assume that the tax and transaction cost related to the transaction is $400,000. Based on this fact pattern, the amount that Drew can invest or spend after the sale of his business is $900,000.

After a sale, Drew would have $1.6 million in liquid assets and $500,000 of real estate. His net worth is $2.1 million but he would no longer have his $220,000 salary and the related benefits. How long will it be before Drew runs out of money in retirement? Based on his lifestyle, he will run out of money before he turns 75. He is frustrated because he feels like he will have to work another 10 years to meet his financial goals. What can Drew do to achieve his retirement dreams?

Improving Your Business Hygiene

In our first illustration, there were a couple of easy first steps that Tim could take in order to become more attractive to the opposite sex: brush his teeth and take a shower. Without these two actions, Tim would never get any dates, no matter how successful and loving he was.

This concept also applies to your business. There are major turnoffs to buyers that are not hard to correct but can make a big difference in attracting suitors. In addition, there are a couple of situations that are such major turnoffs that the business owner must resolve them before placing the business on the market.

Let's stick with the dating analogy. In today's world, Internet dating is very popular. It is unfortunate, but true, that someone on the other side of a computer will size you up in minutes based on your online profile. Your online profile is your first impression to a sea of potential suitors.

First impressions are important. You don't get a date with a bad first impression. For most potential buyers of your business, their first impression of your business is your web site. Remember the last time you searched the Web for a service (house or carpet cleaning, accountant, home improvement, and so on)? I am sure that some web sites were inviting and you wanted to know more about the service, while others were uninspiring and you immediately clicked to the next site.

It is important that you have a web site that will not turn off a buyer. It would be better not to have one than to have a web site that looks like you spent 30 minutes developing it from a 1995 template. Your web site will be the first impression that potential buyers will have about your business. Make sure that it is inviting enough for them to want to pursue you in person.

The second hygiene issue is the look and feel of your business facility. When you are looking to buy a house, "curb appeal" is important. When I am in the market for a house, I know within seconds whether I have interest or not due to "curb appeal." Like a house that is for sale, your business facility projects an image to potential buyers. When potential buyers arrive in person for the first time, does your facility attract them or repel them? How do they feel about your business when they leave? Was it chaotic and sloppy or professional and exciting? Just like a first date, buyers will leave their initial meeting with a specific impression, and it may not accurately reflect the true nature of your business. Before putting your business on the market and having buyers visit your facility, make sure that your facility is clean and organized. Add a fresh coat of paint and new carpet, eliminate the clutter in the office, and get rid of any potential offensive images on your walls.

Consideration   Will having a better web site and a nice-looking and well-organized facility increase the dollars that you get in a sale? Maybe not, but it will increase the number of suitors you will have.

Chapter 4 | Growing Your Value

After potential buyers get past their first impression of your web site and facility, there are other very significant hygiene issues that will have an impact on their desire to pursue your business further. How well your business performs back office tasks (billing, collections, and paying vendors) is very important to buyers. After they buy your business, they want to focus on selling and making a product. They don't want to waste time and energy on the back office issues. The more confidence that buyers have in the efficiency of your back office, the more attractive your business will be to them.

There are a few situations that will make it very difficult for you to sell your business or force you to sell at a fire-sale price. These issues must be resolved before placing your business on the market, and they include a major lawsuit, negative publicity that has been broadcast on the internet or in the media, the loss of a major customer, and defective product and warranty issues. Once you've taken care of those issues, allow some time to elapse from the event before putting your business on the market.

Even if you are not selling your business, addressing these basic business hygiene issues can improve your business's cash flow. An inviting web site will drive business. Cleaning up the facility may allow for productivity gains. A functional back office will allow you to bill and collect receivables quicker. These are important areas to address. However, the real increase in your business value comes from increasing your future cash flows and reducing business risks.

Increasing Your Sustainable Cash Flows

Investors buy future cash flow. They look at your business like it is a cash machine. Any actions taken that increase the future cash flow of your business will increase its value. Investors love to buy cash flow that is repeatable and can grow in the future. There is a three-pronged approach to increasing your sustainable cash flow:

- Increase your revenues.
- Improve your gross margin percentage.
- Lower your operating expenses.

We will discuss strategies on how to increase your revenues and grow your business later in this chapter (see the section on "Developing a Growth Plan"). For now, I will focus on the last two items.

Improve Your Gross Margin Percentage

The most important item on your financial statements to a potential buyer is your gross margin amount and percentage. Gross margin (or gross profit) is the difference between the product selling price and the cost to produce or acquire a product. It measures what is available to you to cover your operating costs and provides you with profits after factoring the costs to make a product. Operating costs include expenses like office wages, rent, advertising, and professional fees. The gross margin percentage is simply the gross margin divided by revenues.

The following is the gross margin level amount and percentage for Sensational Snacks:

Revenues	$ 6,000,000	100.0%
Cost of Goods Sold	4,200,000	70.0%
Gross Margin	$ 1,800,000	30.0%

The cost of goods sold for Sensational Snacks includes the raw materials (potatoes, wheat, cooking oil, and salt) as well as factory wages, facility expenses, equipment costs, and delivery expenses. Determining the cost of goods sold is more difficult for a manufacturer than for a retailer. For a retailer, it is simply the cost to buy the product that is sold to the customer. It is important that you compare your gross margin percentage to others in your industry to see how you stack up. (The best source to find this information is a trade association for your industry.) Also, your gross margin percentage trend is critical when valuing a business. A rising gross margin percentage makes your business more valuable.

There are two ways that you can increase your gross margin percentage. You can either raise the selling price of your products or lower the cost associated with making your products (material and labor):

- *Raise the selling price*: In today's competitive market, it is difficult to raise prices. Price increases across the board do not work. Instead, you should analyze each product or service offered and selectively raise prices on items where demand is strong and competition is weak. Also, you can raise your price if you can increase your customers' perception regarding the value of the product or service that you offer. If you can demonstrate to your customers that your products and services are superior to those of your competitors, then you can charge a premium. Starbucks has been very successful with this strategy. This is how they get customers to pay double for what others charge for a cup of coffee.

Chapter 4 | Growing Your Value

- *Lower the cost of goods sold*: You want to make sure that you are producing or acquiring your products in the most efficient way possible. By lowering your material waste and labor costs, your gross margin percentage will increase. I have seen amazing results from clients who have adopted a Six Sigma or lean approach to making a product or delivering a service. From this, they gained significant efficiencies and have seen their gross margin levels increase. In addition to becoming more efficient, you should carefully study how you purchase raw materials. Lowering the prices you pay for raw material costs will increase your gross margin percentage. You can do this by comparison pricing between vendors, seeking volume discounts, and, in some industries, by using hedging strategies.

You will see increases in your gross margin percentage if you selectively increase prices and become more efficient in delivering your product or service to your customers. A small change in your gross margin percentage will have a large impact on value.

Let's look at how a change in the gross margin impacts Sensational Snacks' value. Drew slightly raises the prices on two of his most popular snack lines. He was also able to reduce product waste and increase his production line efficiency after hiring a lean Six Sigma consultant. Sensational Snacks' gross margin percentage has increased from 30% to 32.5%. After these changes, notice the impact on Sensational Snacks' net income:

Revenues	$ 6,000,000	100.0%
Cost of Goods Sold	4,050,000	67.5%
Gross Margin	1,950,000	32.5%
Operating Expenses	1,300,000	21.7%
Net Income Before Taxes	650,000	10.8%
Income Taxes	227,500	3.8%
Net Income	$ 422,500	7.0%

Drew's gross margin percentage increased from 30% to 32.5% and the gross margin level increased from $1.8 million to $1.95 million. How does this impact his value? Here is the new enterprise value after this change:

Sustainable Net Cash Flow	$ 422,500
Required Rate of Return	25.0%
Enterprise Value	$ 1,690,000

With only an increase of 2.5% in the gross margin percentage, the value of Sensational Snacks increased from $1.3 million to $1.69 million. It was well worth Drew's efforts to focus on improving his gross margin percentage.

Lower Your Operating Expenses

Operating expenses are the costs to operate a business that are not related to producing a product or delivering a service. These costs include office rent, administrative wages, advertising, telephone, utilities, entertainment, and professional fees. Sometimes these costs are called general and administrative expenses or overhead.

It is easier to identify potential cost savings in operating expenses than it is in the cost of goods sold. Looking for the cheapest phone service or coming up with strategies to lower travel costs is much easier than gaining efficiencies at producing a product or delivering a service. Most businesses run a fairly tight ship when it comes to operating expenses. During the recent downturn in the economy, most business owners had to lower their operating expenses in order to survive.

Business owners can become too focused on lowering their operating expenses and hurt their business value down the road. Some operating expenses are necessary to keep you in business (rent, telephone, and office wages), and you should make sure there is no waste in these items. However, there are expenditures that you make that can improve your business value. It makes sense to spend $20,000 on a lean Six Sigma consultant if it will result in a $400,000 increase in the value of your business. Certain expenditures will provide you with a great return on investment including hiring consultants to improve efficiency, preparing annual valuations, and developing a strategic plan. Spend your operating expenses wisely. Cut the expenses that are not needed to keep you in business and that do not increase your business value.

One of the biggest mistakes business owners make is having the business pay for personal expenses. Vacations, vehicle expenses, and relatives on the payroll who do not contribute may provide you with some tax savings, but they also lower your business value. If you are planning on selling during the next few years, I suggest that you forgo those personal perks that you have your business pay. That "business trip" that really was a $30,000 vacation may cost you $120,000 in value. Remember that the price you receive in a sale is a multiple of your cash flow. You may be able to explain to the buyer that the $30,000 business trip was not necessary and should be added back to earnings. Some buyers may agree with you, while others will not. Why risk it? Eliminate personal expenses that are not typical in your business.

Important Do not treat your business like your personal "piggy bank." Avoid having the business pay for your nonbusiness personal expenses. Not only will you sleep better knowing that you are in compliance with the tax law, you will receive more cash proceeds when you sell your business.

Going back to our example, let's see how lowering operating expenses will impact the value of Drew's company. He has decided that the company will no longer have the business pay for all of his vehicles and vacations. In addition, he determined that he was overstaffed by one administrative person and proceeded to eliminate that position. With those two steps, he was able to reduce his operating expenses by $100,000. The following is his revised income statement after improving his gross margin percentage and reducing his operating expenses:

Revenues	$	6,000,000	100.0%
Cost of Goods Sold		4,050,000	67.5%
Gross Margin		1,950,000	32.5%
Operating Expenses		1,200,000	20.0%
Net Income Before Taxes		750,000	12.5%
Income Taxes		263,000	4.4%
Net Income	$	487,000	8.1%

The combination of increased gross margin and reduction of operating expenses has increased his net income from $325,000 to $487,000. Here is the new enterprise value after these two changes:

Sustainable Net Cash Flow	$	487,000
Required Rate of Return		25.0%
Enterprise Value	$	1,948,000

Drew's value just keeps growing. The increase in value due to the increase in the gross margin percentage and lowering operating expenses is $648,000. Certainly it was worth Drew's time and effort to devise strategies to increase his gross margin percentage and lower his operating expenses.

Reducing Your Business Risks

As stated earlier, there is an inverse relationship between your business value and the required rate of return needed to entice an investor to buy your business. The higher rate of return required, the lower the business value. I explained in the previous chapter that the required rate of return is a function of business risk. Business owners must understand this concept. Reducing business risk is the area where I believe business owners have the most control in affecting value. Earlier, I discussed strategies to increase your cash flow; however, the marketplace may prevent a price increase or it may not be possible to reduce your costs to make a product. Business owners can reduce business risk with the proper focus and strategies.

Why does risk lower value? It is because risk causes uncertainty about the future cash flows of the business. Once you truly understand how specific risk factors impact your value, you will be motivated to establish a plan of action to reduce your business risks. The steps involved in reducing your business risks are as follows:

- Identify all of your business risks.
- Quantify how each risk factor impacts your value.
- Prioritize which risk factor you want to focus on.
- Develop strategies and action plans to reduce the risk associated with each risk factor.

Some risk areas will take years to address while others can be minimized by simply purchasing insurance or making the right hire. Based on my experience, the following six areas are the most prevalent risk factors that impact business value:

- *Employee issues:* This is the most common issue that I add a risk premium for. Most privately held businesses have thin management teams and rely on a few employees to drive business performance. The loss of a key employee can significantly impact the company's future cash flow. It is imperative that you build a strong management team and lessen the reliance on any one employee. In order to keep key employees, provide them with market compensation and a long-term incentive plan that rewards their performance. All key employees should have employment and noncompetition agreements. In addition, you may want to buy "key person" life insurance on certain employees. Your most important strategy in this area is to make yourself obsolete. This will significantly lower your risk and provide you with more freedom. If you don't take this step, you will not be able to leave the business when you sell it. The buyer will have to retain you until you can be replaced. This not only reduces your value but will put you in the uncomfortable position of taking orders from someone else. It rarely works out for the seller.

- *Customer concentration:* In Chapter 2, I told the story about a company that had $90 million of its $100 million in revenues with one customer. The company's value vanished when it lost this customer. Besides employee issues, customer concentration is the most common risk factor. The level of the risk premium associated with customer concentration issues depends on the following factors:
  - Is there a long-term contract with the large customer? If so, the risk premium might be reduced.
  - Why does the customer buy from your business? If it is simply based on price and the customer has many alternatives, then the risk premium is higher. If the customer buys because the product or service is unique and hard to duplicate, then the risk premium is lower.
  - How healthy is this customer? Is the company near bankruptcy or financially sound?
  - Does the customer buy based on a relationship with an employee at the business? If so, will the customer stay if that employee leaves the business?

  The buyer or the valuator not only needs to understand the amount of revenues that come from the large customer but also quantify the true risk factor. At times, I have not placed a high risk premium for customer concentration issues. This happens when the risk level is mitigated by a long-term contract or by the fact that the client's product is unique and needed by the customer.

- *Low barriers to entry:* Companies with low barriers to entry are more risky than those with a high barrier to entry. How easy is it for a competitor to enter your market? You may be making a ton of money, but if it is easy for a competitor to grab your market share, it is unlikely that the cash flow will be sustained. A good example of this is web page development companies. In the late 1990s and early 2000s, there were a few large companies that focused on developing web pages for businesses. They did quite well for a few years, but then most of the larger companies in this industry went bankrupt. Why? They created very large organizations with significant overhead, but the cash flow was not sustainable. The barriers

Valuing and Selling Your Business

to entry in the industry were very low. Soon, advertising companies and individuals were competing and the prices to develop web pages dropped significantly. I am not discounting the skill and importance of this service—I'm simply making a point. To get into this business, no license or college education is needed, and there is very little out-of-pocket costs. If you are skilled in this area, all you need to get into business is a computer, a business card, and the ability to market yourself. Compare this to a business that has a significant amount of intellectual property that is protected and requires millions of dollars of investment to get established. There are very few individuals or businesses that have the resources to compete with Apple or MGM casinos.

- *Product sustainability*: Today, products and services become obsolete much faster because of technology advances. If you don't believe this, simply look at the current market value of Research in Motion (the manufacturer of the Blackberry). It is currently worth a fraction of its value five years ago. Why? The iPhone and Android phone technology has displaced the Blackberry. In order to determine the risk level for product sustainability, it is important to perform an analysis of where the company's products are in the life cycle. Are they mature products in a highly competitive market, or is it new technology that is legally protected and will not face major competition in the coming years? To lessen your risk and make your business more valuable, make sure that you protect your products and processes and any other intellectual property legally.

- *Inconsistent financial performance*: Investors love cash flow that is repeatable when making an investment. If there are two companies that have averaged $500,000 a year for the past five years in earnings, which one of the following do you prefer? The one that has earned $500,000 each year for the past five years, or the one that had earned $2 million two of the past five years and lost $500,000 the other three years. Most investors would choose the former. The more volatility that you have in your historical earnings, the higher the risk premium.

Chapter 4 | Growing Your Value

- *Litigation exposure*: Litigation is a fact of life for business owners. This risk area, if managed properly, will not impact the value of a business. It is important that you have the right insurance coverage to protect you from product liability, malpractice, employee issues, and other business risks. A lawsuit against a business that does not have the proper coverage will impact value. The impact level depends on the size of the lawsuit and the probability of a judgment against the business. The same is true for violations against governmental agencies' rules and regulations. A large EPA fine or assessment from the IRS will negatively impact your value. You can lower your risk by being diligent in complying with the governmental agencies that govern your business.

There are many other areas where a risk premium would need to be applied, including the following:

- Too much reliance on one supplier
- Labor availability and strife
- Government regulations that will impact future business
- Negative working capital and other balance weaknesses
- Aggressive actions of your competitors

We have seen Drew increase his value by increasing his gross margin percentage and lowering his operating expenses. Drew has decided to further increase his value by reducing the risk associated with his business. The first thing he does is to establish a plan to make himself obsolete in the business. He hires a corporate psychologist to assess the leadership abilities of his management team. It is determined that his daughter has the ability and desire to take over Drew's CEO role. She enrolls in an executive MBA program and hires a works with the psychologist to expedite her progress. In addition, the sales manager and the plant manager sign employment and noncompetition agreements. With these changes, buyers will feel more comfortable that the business could survive without Drew. In addition, they will not worry about his key employees leaving and competing. With these changes, the required rate of return needed to entice a buyer is reduced from 25% to 20%. The following shows the impact on value with this risk reduction:

Sustainable Net Cash Flow	$ 487,000	$ 487,000
Required Rate of Return	25.0%	20.0%
Enterprise Value	$ 1,948,000	$ 2,435,000

A change from a 25% required rate of return to 20% has made a big impact on value. The value has increased by $487,000! Drew is motivated to reduce his other major risk. He decides to no longer be so dependent on one customer. He hires an aggressive sales person who develops new markets and customers for his products. In addition, he stops selling his low margin products to his 30% customer. This combination reduces the largest customer's sales to 15% of total revenues, and the top three customers now comprise only 30% of the revenues. By doing this, Sensational Snacks' profits are no longer at the mercy of the three largest customers' whims and demands and Drew's earnings are more repeatable. By lowering his customer concentration and making his earnings more repeatable, Drew has reduced the required rate of return to 15%.

What is the value of Sensational Snacks assuming a 15% required rate of return?

Sustainable Net Cash Flow	$	487,000
Required Rate of Return		15.0%
Enterprise Value	$	3,247,000

Drew's hard work to reduce his business risks has really paid off. The value of Sensational Snacks has increased from $1.95 million to $3.25, million with the reduction of the required rate of return from 25% to 15%. The required rate of return reduction is due to Drew proactively reducing the company's reliance on himself and the one large customer.

Important Business owners should identify the risk factors associated with their business and have specific strategies and action plans in their strategic plan to reduce these business risks.

Developing a Growth Plan

The buyer's perception of your future growth rate will impact the value of your business. The higher the expected growth rate, the higher the value of your business. You can increase the value of your business by developing a strategy to have sustainable profitable growth.

The compound annual growth rate (CAGR) measures the annual growth of a business over a certain period of time. What is most important is the buyer's perception of future growth. The best way to improve that perception is to have a few years of CAGR higher than others in your industry. There is no better combination than a high historical growth CAGR and the expectation of continued growth. In a hot industry, growth is easier than a mature market. Most industries are mature, and growth has to come from taking business away from competitors or developing new products.

Of course, growth can come from buying another company. If you have a strong desire to grow quickly, this may be a good strategy for you. Is it better to buy growth or to have organic growth? Growth through acquisition can be an effective strategy if you don't overpay and have a well thought-out implementation strategy. In most surveys about business transactions, less than 50% of acquirers are happy with the results of an acquisition. Why is that? They either overpaid or did not properly integrate the acquired business into their existing business.

When clients engage me to assist them in buying a business, I tell them to spend as much time in developing integration plans as they do in the pursuit of the deal. It is sort of like getting married. Many spend more time planning their wedding than figuring out how to live together in harmony for the rest of their lives.

Which should you pursue: organic growth or an acquisition? With some analysis, you will be able to answer this question. If your business has an opportunity to buy a company for $1 million, would you be better off buying it or spending $1 million trying to duplicate what you are buying? Prepare an analysis to determine the answer. Many are surprised by the end result and forgo their acquisitions plans, putting all their efforts into organic growth.

With the recent worldwide economic downturn, there is a hunt for growth for most companies. Growth is hard to find. What can you do to increase your chances of obtaining sustainable growth? There are three basic growth strategies to consider:

- *Market penetration*: This involves selling more of your products and services into your existing market. You develop a plan to obtain more customers through advertising, efforts of your sales force and channel partners, or price reductions. This is the easiest strategy to develop but usually does not create sustainable profitable growth. You are essentially just stealing customers from your competitors. The other problem with this strategy is that sales growth may come at the expense of your gross margin. You create value by increasing your gross margin percentage. Getting into price wars to gain market share lowers your gross margin percentage.

- *Product development*: For many, the best way to increase revenues is to develop new products or services that you can sell to your existing customers. Apple is the master at this strategy. Many of my friends have four or five Apple products and will buy the next thing that the company sells whether they need it or not. This can be much more profitable than stealing customers from your competitors.

However, it comes with more risk and will cost you time and money to develop new products and services that may not be accepted in the marketplace. It is imperative that you spend a significant amount of time and analysis in determining if the marketplace really wants your new product or service before using this strategy.

- *Market development:* This strategy entails expanding your geographic reach, including international sales. With the advent of the Internet, this strategy is now available to many more businesses. You need to perform a good cost-benefit analysis before committing to this strategy. If it will cost you $300,000 to open up a new office in a different location, how much product do you have to sell in order to break even? Will you become distracted by the new location and lose focus? Can you maintain the same quality control in a different location? These questions need to be answered before proceeding with this strategy.

Buyers are attracted to you when you have a growth strategy you can articulate and there is traction in moving that strategy forward. They also are impressed when you are able to show them that you have a firm grasp about your marketplace. You should know what your market share is and, more importantly, your potential market share.

The final piece of increasing Sensational Snacks' value is to implement a growth strategy. Drew develops a strategy to add a gourmet potato chip line and sells it to existing customers. It has been accepted by some of his customers and will increase his revenues by $300,000. The following is the new income statement after all of the changes discussed have been implemented. His net income has increased from $325,000 to $551,000.

Revenues	$ 6,300,000	100.0%
Cost of Goods Sold	4,253,000	67.5%
Gross Margin	2,047,000	32.5%
Operating Expenses	1,200,000	19.0%
Net Income Before Taxes	847,000	13.4%
Income Taxes	296,000	4.7%
Net Income	$ 551,000	100.0%

The long-term expected growth rate has increased by 1%, which lowers the rate of return required by an investor to 14%. The value of Sensational Snacks with these changes is as follows:

Sustainable Net Cash Flow	$	551,000
Required Rate of Return		14.0%
Enterprise Value	$	3,936,000

Drew's Newfound Freedom

The combination of increasing cash flows, lowering business risk, and increasing sustainable growth is very powerful. Sensational Snacks is now worth $3.94 million which is over three times the original value.

Can Drew retire? Assuming a tax and transaction cost of 30% of the enterprise value, Drew's net proceeds from the sale of his business would be $2.76 million. His liquid assets have increased from $700,000 to $3.46 million. This along with his $500,000 of real estate brings his net worth close to $4 million. Now he is able to retire at the lifestyle that he wants, but he is unsure if he wants to retire. He enjoys going to work more than ever and may put off retirement for a couple of years. Instead, he will fund his retirement with the additional profits, making it possible to gift or sell the business to his kids at a bargain price. By treating his business "like an investment" and increasing its value, he no longer feels stuck and has many different options to choose from.

Before concluding this chapter, I would like to make one last point in making your business more attractive to potential suitors. If you are thinking about selling your business in the next five years, it is important to make your business look as professional as possible.

Professionalizing Your Business

What does it mean to professionalize your business? It is simply giving the impression to a buyer that your business has the look and feel of a well-oiled machine. It provides buyers with additional confidence that they are making the right decision to buy your business. It also protects the value that you worked so hard to create. It is tragic when a business owner has developed a great business model but then sees value destroyed by not paying attention to certain areas of the business There are six main areas that will make your business more professional and more attractive to a buyer:

- *Upgrade your accounting and legal service*: Which provides a suitor more comfort—financial records in a shoebox or an audit from a large reputable CPA firm? Business owners thinking about selling their business should have an outside accounting firm provide them with either reviewed or audited financial statements. An audit provides the highest level of assurance and a review is the next step down. It is also important to engage a seasoned business lawyer to review and update your buy-sell, employment agreements, customer contracts, and other important agreements. Many business owners have the same CPA and lawyer whom they started with. Make sure that the professionals on your team are the best ones to get you through the selling process. It may not be your golfing buddy or your spouse's cousin who will be effective at making this happen.

- *Employee manuals and job descriptions*: A buyer wants to be confident that the business will continue to be profitable after a transaction. It is not unusual for there to be some turnover of employees once a transaction occurs. What creates the future cash flow? Employees! Buyers feel better about buying a business that has employee roles and responsibilities well documented. This makes it easier to replace someone and keep the cash machine moving forward. The more roles and procedures that are documented, the more assurance buyers will have when they buy your business.

- *Compliance with government regulators*: This includes complying with the IRS, EPA, and Equal Opportunity Employment practices and meeting governmental worker safety standards. A serious violation with any of these could cost your business hundreds of thousands of dollars and perhaps your entire business.

- *Proper internal controls to prevent theft*: Each year, I hear about a trusted employee who stole hundreds of thousands of dollars. Recently, a client shared with me how a major theft had been discovered by accident. His payroll clerk got into a serious auto accident on payday. She tried to escape from the ambulance because she had placed a friend who did not work for the business on the payroll (a ghost employee). The owner figured it out when he had to hand out the paychecks due to her accident. It is important that you have the proper internal controls in place and be insured against theft.

- *Effective corporate governance*: Having an outside board of directors and/or an advisory board will provide you with an important sounding board. When the right people are chosen, they can provide you with solid business advice and help you avoid a major loss in value. Many business owners regret making major decisions without some additional advice and oversight.

- *Identify and document your intangible assets:* Intangible assets are critical to the success of all businesses. You want to make sure that buyers understand what they are buying when they purchase your business. They will know that they are buying inventory, fixed assets, receivables, and some intangibles (e.g., customers and patents). However, many intangible assets are much harder to identify. You need to communicate to a buyer all of your intangible assets that your business owns, such as the following:
  - Market research you've conducted
  - Processes and formulas for making products
  - Your approach to customer service
  - The relationships you have in the community and industry
  - Experienced employees
  - Proprietary products and processes
  - Proprietary software that you have developed

  It is worth your effort to document your intangible assets and legally protect the ones that you can (patents, trademarks, and copyrights). Products and ideas that are unique and provide you with a competitive advantage should be protected from outsiders through patents, trademarks, and other means. An idea stolen that is not protected can cause serious damage to your business.

Summary

There are ways you can make your business more valuable and attractive to potential suitors. Hopefully, the end result of what happened to Sensational Snacks has provided you with some motivation to develop plans to increase your business value. There are three key areas that you can focus on to increase your business value:

- Increase your sustainable cash flow.
- Reduce your business risks.
- Develop a growth plan.

As part of your strategic plan, develop strategies and action plans in each of these three key areas. Small changes can make a big difference in your business value. Also, improve your business hygiene and make your company look more professional and protect your value. You will attract more potential buyers, which will drive up the price of your business.

In the next chapter, I will walk you through the process of selling of your business from the time you decide to place your business on the market to the closing of the deal.

CHAPTER 5

Selling Your Business

Who Will Get Your Baby?

"Bruce, this is the last client that I will act as an intermediary for in selling a business." I wish I would have said that one project earlier.

In 1999, my partner and I decided to expand our consulting practice to include the service of selling businesses for a success fee. The majority of our fees were based on whether we successfully located a buyer for our clients' businesses.

The experience that I gained providing this service was invaluable and has enabled me to provide better advice to business owners about how buyers value their business and the selling process. This is because of the experience in dealing with the realities of the marketplace, I now advise my clients from "real-world" experience instead of a merely academic point of view.

We closed many deals, and it was a high-risk, high-reward service offering. When a business sold and the seller received the price that he wanted, everyone was happy and we got paid a lucrative fee. Other times, we spent a significant amount of time and resources on a deal that was never consummated and we did not receive a success fee. Most of the time, deals did not close because we did not find the right buyer willing to pay the price the seller wanted. Other times, we found the right buyer at the right price, but the sellers backed away at the last minute because they were not emotionally ready to sell. When we sold a business, we obtained a fee that was significantly higher than a consulting fee based on our hourly rates. Of course, if a deal did not close, the opposite happened. The feast-or-famine fee arrangement was frustrating in that it provided unpredictable income.

I knew providing this service was risky. When people buy a business for millions and it doesn't work out the way they hoped, they like to point fingers. Usually, they don't point their fingers at their own decisions.

When I reluctantly agreed to take on the engagement, I did not realize it was going to be part of my life for seven years and that I would be a defendant in a lawsuit for the first time in my life.

The lawsuit was settled a couple of years ago, so it is very fresh in my mind. We were sued three years and eleven months after the deal closed. The statute of limitations for professional services in Ohio is four years. Because of a confidentiality agreement, I cannot provide you with specific details of the engagement, but I will give you with an overview and describe the crux of the case.

The company that we represented was in the housing industry and was very successful. The deal closed in the winter of 2007, only a couple of weeks before the collapse of the housing market. The sellers that we represented started a similar type of business in the western part of the United States and decided they wanted sell their business and focus on their new companies.

The engagement started about one year before closing. We received a *letter of intent* (LOI) from the eventual buyer within weeks of being engaged by the sellers. Once the LOI was accepted, the buyer proceeded to perform due diligence over the next 60 days. The due diligence process did not go very well. The buyer came back and said he found many things that caused him concern and would agree to buy our client's company at a significantly reduced price. My client was not too thrilled with the reduction in price, and we tabled the deal for a few months. A few months later, we reopened negotiations and the parties eventually agreed on a price. The attorneys then went to work on an asset purchase agreement and after a few hiccups, the deal eventually closed.

Within 90 days of the deal closing, the sellers were informed by the buyer's attorney that they had violated the clause in the asset purchase agreement about providing accurate financial statements. The sellers provided financial data for a four-year period as an exhibit in the asset purchase agreement. The buyer claimed that one number was materially wrong on the latest financial statement provided. These statements were prepared by the sellers' internal accountant and were not reviewed or audited by an outside accountant. We made it clear to the buyer that we did not provide any assurance about their financial records and that the buyer needed to conduct his own due diligence. The buyer hired a financial expert to examine the company's financial records.

The buyers sued the seller to recover the monies held in escrow and demanded a good portion of the purchase price back. After a couple of years of battle, the sellers declared bankruptcy. The housing industry collapsed, and the epicenter of the collapse was the location where the sellers started their new business and invested the funds from the sale. Their personal fortunes were gone. During the lawsuit against our client, our records were subpoenaed and I was deposed. After it was clear that nothing could be recovered from the sellers, the buyer proceeded to sue us to recover his claims of damages. The discovery period lasted almost two years, including a dozen depositions in five different states. It was a very time consuming and emotionally draining process. Fortunately, I had a great support system with my family, friends and fellow partners at Rea & Associates—for which I am forever grateful.

My intention is not to scare you off from selling your business. I was involved with many deals that went very well and where both the buyer and seller achieved their goals, including those where the seller received tens of millions of dollars. It is very fulfilling to be part of the process that assists business owners in selling their business to the right buyer, enabling them move on to the next phase in life.

Selling your business will be one of the most difficult things that you will ever do. It is complex and time-consuming and will be hard on you emotionally. The perspectives that you will receive in this chapter come from both the "thrill of victory" related to successful deals and the "agony of defeat" regarding the ones that did not go so well.

There are two important decisions that you need to make preliminary to selling your business. The first is, "When is the best time to sell the business?" The second is, "Who is the best buyer?" The next two sections discuss these two decisions before turning to the "ins and outs" of the selling process.

The Best Time to Sell Your Business

The majority of business owners will eventually sell their business. Few will give it away to family members or simply shut down the business when they exit. With this in mind, when is the best time to sell your business? If the following is all lined up perfectly, you will be able to sell your business at the optimal price:

- Your sustainable cash flow has peaked.
- Your business risks are at the lowest level.
- Your forecasted growth is at its highest level.
- Bankers are lending money freely at great interest rates.
- The overall economy is doing well.
- Income taxes on business transactions are favorable.
- There are buyers available that have significant cash levels.
- There is aggressive buying of companies in your industry.
- You are able to find fulfillment and sense of purpose outside the business.

If all these factors are aligned perfectly for you today and you want out, don't hesitate. Place your business on the market and reap your rewards!

But it's not as easy as it seems. I have seen everything aligned perfectly for an industry only once in my career. This was in the late 1990s for the technology industry. The economy was humming, the infancy of the Internet was driving growth and profits to record levels, and there were irrational buyers in the marketplace. Companies were buying others based on multiples of revenues and not profits. The sellers were becoming millionaires though their companies had never achieved a profit. Then someone woke up and questioned the valuations of all the technology companies. The stock market crashed, and the economy slowed down. Timing is an important consideration when selling your business.

You cannot always predict swings in the market, and some factors are beyond your control in optimizing the timing for selling your business. These factors include current macroeconomic conditions, interest rates, industry trends, and buyer activity. Selling a business isn't just about trying to time the market—it's about timing your business.

You should therefore be diligent at all times in growing your business value and not be so worried about the general economic factors outside of your control. If you do this, then you can try to time the market to optimize your price.

This constant state of readiness also allows you to obtain a better price for your business should an unfortunate circumstance such as illness enter your life that forces you to sell the business sooner than you desired. There are other reasons why you may want to sell your business sooner than later. If you hate going to work everyday and are completely burnt out, it is time to get out—if only because you will not be able to focus on increasing the value of your business and may make serious mistakes that detract from its value. Alternatively, if you have reason to expect that over the next few years your earnings will decrease significantly due to circumstances out of your control, you may want to consider "cashing out" sooner than later.

Important Concentrate on growing the value of your business while understanding how outside factors impact the best time to sell your business. This will allow you to maximize the price you will receive for your business.

The Best Buyer for Your Business

Now to the question of who is the preferred buyer? There are two broad categories of buyers of businesses: *synergistic* and *financial*. Synergistic buyers are larger companies (usually competitors) in your industry and will pay you more for your business because they can achieve higher cash flows than you can through cost reductions (layoffs of employees) or increased margins. The financial buyer will continue the business in its present form. A financial buyer can be someone inside your business, a family member, or an outside investor.

You will have to decide whether obtaining top dollar for your business or continuing your legacy is more important. You rarely accomplish both of these goals with one buyer. Once you choose which type of buyer is the best for you, a strategy can be developed to find the right buyer. The following is a summary of the types of buyers and tips for selecting the best buyer for your business.

Selling to a Synergistic Buyer

Although the synergistic buyer option will provide the highest price, the number of synergistic buyers is limited and this option is not available to all business owners. You will want to consider selling to a synergistic buyer if you are in one of the following situations:

- *Obtaining the highest price is most important to you*: Many start a business to become rich. This strategy will provide the highest selling price for you. If you are concerned about your legacy or the future of your employees, then another option may be better.

- *You have a retirement shortfall*: You may not like the idea of selling to a competitor or other synergistic buyer, but it may be the only way to meet your retirement needs.

- *The price received would provide a windfall that secures your family for life*: I have been involved in deals where the business owner obtains tens of millions of dollars. They are able to provide financial security for their entire family for life and support charities they love. You may want your children to take your business, but it is hard to pass up an offer that secures your children's financial future and allows them to pursue other endeavors.

Selling to an ESOP

An *employee stock ownership plan* (ESOP) is a qualified retirement plan for the employees of a company.[1] If you sell your stock to an ESOP, it probably will be at a lower price than selling it to a synergistic buyer. However, you could end

---

[1] It is not in the scope of this book to fully explain what ESOPs are and the advantages and disadvantages of them. For further information please visit http://www.nceo.org/

up with more after-tax proceeds. This is because you will have the opportunity to defer paying taxes from the gain of the sale of your stock to an ESOP. In order for this to happen, the proceeds must be reinvested in certain domestic investments (see IRS section 1042 for specifics). ESOPs are not easy to establish and can be costly to maintain. They are only possible if you have a strong management team that is able to operate your business once you leave. You will want to consider selling your stock to an ESOP if you are in one of the following situations:

- *You desire to preserve the culture once you leave:* This is a good option if you want to preserve both jobs and the culture you created. Outside buyers will run the business as they wish and may make changes you will not like. By selling it to your employees, it is more likely that your philosophy and legacy will continue than if you sell it to outsiders.

- *You want to reward your employees:* Some business owners sell their business to an ESOP because they appreciate all the efforts their employees have made to their success and want to reward them with ownership.

Selling to a Financial Buyer

Most business transactions are to a financial buyer that is not part of the business. There is a large universe of financial buyers, but they are hard to identify. Financial buyers can range from private equity groups to local corporate executives who have lost their jobs. They may be experienced buyers or complete novices. You will want to consider this option when the following apply to your situation:

- *A synergistic buyer is not available:* If you cannot attract a synergistic buyer and do not want to pursue an ESOP, then this option will provide you with the highest price. This is particularly true if there is competition among financial buyers for your business.

- *You do not want a synergistic buyer:* You may wish to preserve your culture and maintain jobs, but selling to family members or employees is not an option. Try to locate a financial buyer that has similar values and philosophy. If this is important to you, spend considerable amount of time with the buyer to make sure he or she is the right person to continue your legacy once you leave.

Selling to an Insider

Selling to your children, other family members, and/or key employees will provide you with the lowest amount of cash at closing compared with the other selling options. Most of the time, your children and employees will not have the financial resources needed to buy a business. Therefore, the amount of cash received at closing will be less than other options and you will have to finance a large part of the purchase price. Consider this strategy if the following is important to you:

- *Your children own the business but not as a gift*: You don't need the money but want your kids to buy the business as a matter of principle. You may believe it is better for their children's character that they have to buy the business with their own resources, or it is a fairness issue with your other children.

- *You want an insider to own the business, but you do not have enough for your retirement*: Some parents sell the business to their children because they need the sale proceeds to retire. Consider this option if you want an insider to own the business, but you need more resources to retire.

- *You would like to continue to show up to work*: If you sell the business to insiders, they may let you keep the keys to the front door and even ask you for your advice. When you sell it to an unrelated party, the new owners probably will make you turn in your keys, shake your hand, and wish you the best of luck.

You have spent a lot of blood, sweat, and tears in starting and operating your business. It is not an easy process of turning over the keys of your baby to someone else. It is important that you understand the advantages and disadvantages of each of these buyers and make a decision as to which type of buyer you would like to pursue.

Discuss these options with your spouse, kids, and trusted advisors. Each buyer type requires a different strategy and focus. For example, if you want to sell to an ESOP, you will have to have a strong management team; whereas a synergistic buyer might have key employees who will move into your business once the transaction is complete.

The Terms of the Deal

Selling a business is unlike any transaction that you have ever experienced. The largest transaction that most people have been involved with is real estate. Selling your house can be complex, but it is child's play compared with selling

Chapter 5 | Selling Your Business

a business. The price and cash you receive from selling your house are easy to comprehend. There is a closing statement that spells it all out. Also, it is clear what is being sold: your house and specific contents that have been identified in the simple three-page real estate contract. The same cannot be said about a business transaction.

When you sell your business, you will come to an agreement on the price for the business with the buyer. The next question to ask is this—how will the price be paid? It is rare when it is similar to a real estate purchase in that 100% of the price is paid at closing. The typical components of the payment for a business include the following:

- The majority of the price is paid in cash at closing.
- A portion of the price is held in escrow.
- The seller may finance a portion of the deal by accepting a note from the buyer.
- The price may increase due to an earn-out clause.
- A consulting, noncompete and employment agreement is often included.

As a seller of your business, you want as much of the deal price as possible to be in cash at closing. The buyer wants the amount of cash paid at closing to be as little as possible. The amount paid at closing is part of the deal negotiations.

It is typical that a portion of the deal price will be placed in escrow to allow for a reduction in the price after closing for either a violation of the purchase agreement or buying an asset in which value is in question (e.g., the true value of accounts receivable). The amount placed in escrow is typically 10% to 20% of the purchase price for a 90- to 180-day period. The funds are held by an independent escrow agent and will be released to the seller once the buyer gives the escrow agent approval to release the funds.

Most buyers like the seller to have some "skin in the game" after they sell the business and to remain financially attached to the deal. This can be accomplished by a seller's note, an earn-out and a covenant not to compete.

- *Seller's note*: Many times, the seller will have to finance part of the purchase price. Buyers may need to bridge the gap between the purchase price and their own resources and the amount the bank will lend on the deal. The note covers the difference. The seller's note is subordinate to bank financing, and you should always try to secure the note to a buyer's reachable asset. I warn my clients to have the mindset that they may not collect the entire value of the note; thus, they should make all their financial plans based on cash received at closing. The note should not exceed 20% of the purchase price.

- *Earn-out*: An earn-out is the portion of the purchase price that is paid after closing based on reaching certain milestones previously agreed upon. This means the ultimate purchase price can increase if the buyer meets the goals spelled out in the earn-out. An earn-out is used when there is a valuation gap that needs to be bridged or when there is a large risk factor that concerns the buyer. For example, in Chapter 2, we discussed the client that had 90% of its revenues from one customer. A possible earn-out in that scenario is that a large portion of the purchase price is contingent on that main customer remaining for a specified time period.

  Often, the buyer and seller cannot come to an agreement on the ultimate purchase price, but they would like to move forward. An earn-out gives sellers the ability to achieve the price they want and provides buyers some assurance that they have not overpaid. Performance-based earn-outs may be based on revenues, gross profits, EBITDA, or net income. I prefer that earn-outs be based on revenues or gross profits since the EBITDA and net income levels are subject to manipulation by the buyer. Early in my career, I was an expert in a litigation case where the buyer and seller had an earn-out arrangement based on the EBITDA levels. The seller never collected on that earn-out because the buyer proceeded to take out a $1 million salary and there were no profits left in the company to pay the earn-out.

- *Covenant not to compete*: In the majority of business deals, the seller is required to sign a covenant, as part of the transaction, not to compete. Most buyers would never buy a business if the seller could collect cash at closing and open up a competing business across the street. There usually is a separate value assigned to the covenant promising not to compete and is considered part of the total deal package. In addition, the seller may receive either a consulting agreement or an employment agreement as part of the deal. The buyer will want the seller's expertise to assist in the transition process. Sometimes, this is included in the purchase price, and other times it is a separate contract signed at closing. Buyers like to shift some of the purchase price to a consulting agreement for tax purposes

What Are You Selling?

The answer to this question seems to be simple: your business! But it's not that simple. Will you be selling your company's stock or business assets? Will all of the business assets transfer to the buyer or just the goodwill, inventory, and equipment? Which party is responsible for the company's liabilities? These questions will be answered during the negotiation process and documented in the purchase agreement.

As a seller, you will want to sell your company's stock (stock deal) because you will then relieve yourself from any obligations that may arise from the past. Plus, there is a huge tax advantage. However, the buyer typically does not want to buy your stock but would rather buy business assets and assume as few of your liabilities as possible (asset deal). During my career, about 95% of sales transactions have been asset deals.

In a stock deal, the shares of stock of the business are transferred from the seller to the buyer, as well as all of the assets, liabilities, and operations. Also, any skeletons that may arise from the past (i.e., tax issues, product warranty, employee suits) will be the buyer's responsibility. There are major tax disadvantages for the buyer in a stock deal. The business assets depreciate in the same manner as they did before the transaction, but at a rate that is lower than it would be under an asset deal. Also, the buyer is not able to write off any of the purchase price as a tax deduction. In a stock transaction, the buyer assumes more risks and has a significant tax disadvantage. It is rare when you find a buyer who is willing to do that.

In an asset deal, the seller retains ownership of the stock of the company. The buyer must either create a new entity or use another existing entity for the transaction. Only assets and liabilities that are specifically identified in the purchase agreement are transferred to the buyer. Other than some specified liabilities, such as accounts payables and lease obligations, all other liabilities of the company remain with the seller. This means if a lawsuit arises from an event prior to the closing of the deal, sellers will have to defend themselves out of their own funds. After selling the business under an asset deal, the seller liquidates the business entity and then receives the proceeds personally. Buyers record the assets and liabilities at the fair market value assigned to them as part of the transaction. This allows buyers to have greater annual depreciation of the fixed assets purchased, which lowers their income taxes. Unlike a stock transaction, the buyer will be able to write off any value assigned to goodwill as well as any other intangible assets over a 15-year period.

The seller's tax consequence under an asset deal is usually much higher than under a stock deal. Sometimes the difference is significant. Because of the importance of this topic, we will discuss this further with an example at the end of this chapter.

The Steps in Selling Your Business

The process of selling your business is more complex, emotionally draining, and time consuming than selling a house. It is important that you are mentally ready for the uncertainty and stress that goes along with it. Have a timeline in your mind for when you would like to sell your business, but be flexible. Find someone you can trust who has either been through the process or has assisted others that you can talk with confidentially and openly while you are selling your business.

The following is the typical order of events that occur once you decide to place your business on the market:

- Select your transaction team.
- Locate the buyer.
- Sign a letter of intent.
- Enter the due diligence process.
- Negotiate the asset purchase agreement.
- Close the deal.

Before placing your business on the market, you want to be able to articulate your reasons for selling and you should also consider telling your key employees.

Many owners are reluctant to tell their key employees that they are selling the business. They fear these employees will run out the door searching for a new job if they hear that the business is for sale. One client told me that his biggest concern about placing his business on the market was that his employees would find out. He and his wife were 80 years old and frail. But actually, the employees were scared he would not sell the business and that it would be liquidated after his death.

I believe that it's important that you inform your key employees of your intentions. They will likely sense that something is going on. Rumor and innuendo can make them leave faster than hearing the truth. Articulate why you are selling, assure them that you will tell the buyer how important they are to the business, and properly incentivize them to stay. The incentive that is popular in this situation is a large retention bonus that is paid to the employee(s) after the deal is closed.

Can you state your reasons for selling? Prospective buyers will want to know your reasons. Planned retirement or wanting to cash out and accept a new challenge in your life are some of the best reasons for selling. This provides some comfort to the buyer that there are no hidden business reasons for selling the business. Whatever the reason, make sure you can confidently explain it since buyers naturally wonder—if the business is so great, why are you selling?

> **Important** Keep the end in mind during the selling process. You are exiting for a reason so don't let your emotions derail you from your financial and personal goals. Find someone you can trust during the process to be a sounding board and provide you with an objective perspective.

Select Your Transaction Team

It is important that you select the right advisors to be on your team. Once the deal is closed, there is no turning back. For most, this will be the largest and most complex transaction that they will be a part of in their lifetime. You will need trusted, experienced advisors to assist you and be able to provide you with their full attention. Figure 5-1 shows which advisors are needed and how they interact with each other:

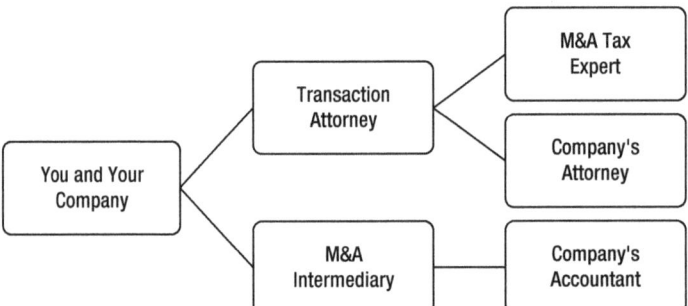

Figure 5-1. These experts are needed for an M&A transaction to allow the best chance for success

Before placing your business on the market, obtain an independent valuation that provides you with a value both for an investment value standard (synergistic buyer) and a fair market value standard (financial buyer). This valuation will provide you with some assurance of the validity of the offers you receive. You want someone independent providing you with the valuation and not the intermediary whose compensation is tied to the sale of the business.

The person whom you hire to find the buyer and quarterback the process has many different names in the business community, including *investment banker*, *business broker*, and *intermediary*. Investment bankers typically handle very large transactions (in excess of $100 million), whereas business brokers deal with smaller transactions ($1 million or less). M&A intermediaries handle transactions in the middle, though both brokers and investment bankers sometimes dip into this territory as well. Throughout this chapter, I am going to use the term *intermediary* to mean the advisor who will quarterback the process. The intermediary receives a *retainer* or a *commitment fee* to initiate the selling process and will also receive a *success fee* if a transaction consummates, and they will want an exclusive arrangement for 6 to 12 months.

The intermediary has many different roles in the selling process. His main job is to find the right buyer for you, quarterback the entire process, and be the buffer zone between you and the buyer. It is a critical role. You want this person to create competition among buyers to drive up the price in a confidential way. Intermediaries need excellent communication and problem-solving skills and the patience of a marriage counselor. After obtaining an LOI, the intermediary will work closely with you and your accountant in the due diligence process. When you move to the purchase agreement, they will work in conjunction with the transaction attorney to make sure the agreement aligns with your wishes.

Hiring an intermediary is a good idea when you don't know who the buyer may be or if there are a number of known potential buyers. If you don't need someone to assist you in locating buyers and you know who the buyer of your business will be, then an experienced valuation professional or a CPA may be sufficient to assist you through the selling process. One of the most important roles of a professional assisting you in the selling process is to serve as a buffer between you and the buyer. Buyers want to have their questions answered and be able to express their concerns about the business to someone. This does not make for good conversation with the seller. I have seen many deals go sour because the seller had direct conversations with the buyer.

The *transaction attorney* has an equally important role: to let you sleep at night after the deal is closed. Studies have shown that less than 50% of buyers are satisfied with an M&A transaction. There are various reasons why so many are dissatisfied—they may believe they paid too much for the business or that they did not fully understand how the business operated. They may also feel that they were misled by the seller regarding the health of the business.

Even if you disclosed everything possible and the buyer had complete access to all materials, there is still a chance that the buyer will try to negotiate a lower purchase price or try to recover some of the proceeds paid to you. The transaction attorney's role is to document your wishes in the purchase agreement and to limit your exposure to future litigation or recovery of funds once the deal has closed. They will work closely with your corporate attorney to ensure all legal issues have been disclosed. They also will work with the M&A tax expert to ensure the purchase agreement properly documents the tax treatment of the transaction. If the IRS ever questions the tax treatment of the deal, they will use the signed purchase agreement as the starting point in their investigation.

Finally, you will want to retain an expert in the M&A tax field. You need someone who really understands M&A tax issues and has years of experience. As you will see later in this chapter, a mistake in how taxes are treated in an M&A transaction can cost you dearly.

Remind your advisors that they work for you. Deals can get derailed if attorneys and other professionals have their egos hurt during the M&A process. When it gets nasty, they could easily lose sight of their client's goal.

Critical   Make sure that the professionals on your team understand their role and that their job is to accomplish your ultimate goal—a successful sale. You are the one in control of this process.

Locate the Buyer

Once you choose which type of buyer is the best for you, you can develop a strategy to find the right buyer. If the buyer is outside of your company, you should work closely with the intermediary on developing this strategy. If you know that the buyer is an internal buyer, there is no need to hire an intermediary.

The intermediary will develop a marketing plan and send out a "teaser" about your business to develop interest. The teaser should not disclose your identity and should be discrete. Make sure that you review what is being sent out about your company to potential buyers.

Hopefully, the intermediary will have a robust response to this initial marketing campaign. The intermediary should screen potential buyers before providing them with any additional information. The screening process includes making sure the buyer is financially sound. Nothing is more frustrating than to spend months on a deal and find out that the buyer is not able to close the transaction due to lack of funds. You may want to screen out specific companies or individuals to whom you don't feel comfortable giving access to your financial information. This could be your biggest competitor or someone who bought your friend's company and did not keep his promises.

Once you are confident that the potential buyer has adequate financing and you feel comfortable with releasing financial information about your company, the prospective buyer should sign a confidentiality agreement. It is important that your corporate attorney reviews the confidentiality agreement to make sure it protects you. After the buyer signs the confidentiality agreement, the intermediary will send the buyer a *confidential information memorandum* (CIM). This document not only discloses your identity but includes a summary about your operations, historical financial results, and your prospects for the future.

The purpose of the CIM is to obtain an offer from a prospective buyer. Hopefully, you will have several offers to choose from and you will receive an LOI that meets your satisfaction.

Suggestion "Date" the buyer before making any commitments. Spend a lot of time with the buyer to make sure this is the right person to take over your baby.

Sign a Letter of Intent

Once a buyer is found, it is time for the engagement period. The prospective groom gives his future bride the promise of a great life and his commitment with a ring. A buyer does the same thing with the term sheet or the LOI. Term sheets and LOIs are both preliminary, nonbinding documents that record an agreement between the parties on the major terms of a deal. The difference between the two is simply a matter of style. A term sheet lists the deal terms in bullet-point format, and an LOI is written in letter form. I will use the latter term in this chapter. These key components are a part of this agreement:

- Specifics of what is being purchased, including whether the transaction is an asset or stock deal
- Price and final pay-out at closing
- Agreement about any seller financing or earn-out
- Details of the due diligence process
- Removal of the seller from the market
- Proposal for a closing date

After you sign the LOI, you lose your negotiating power. The price and terms you agreed to in the LOI will not get any better and can become less favorable. During the due diligence process, if buyers find items they do not like, they may try to renegotiate the deal. I have never seen a case where the buyer says, "The business is better than we expected so we are going to offer you more money!"

For a specified period of time, you will have to honor a "no shop" agreement and take your business off the market. However, you don't want the trail to get too cold if there are other interested parties. You need to limit the due diligence process and have the "no shop" agreement become void immediately if the buyer intends to materially change any deal terms. Give buyers a specific time period (less than 60 days) to perform their financial due diligence. I advise sellers to have a meeting with the buyer within 30 days of starting the due diligence process to determine if the buyer has any intention of changing the terms.

■ **Land mine** Don't sign an LOI until your attorney has reviewed it and you are completely satisfied with all deal terms. The deal will not get any better, and you can lose out on other interested parties if you sign an LOI with a buyer who will not honor the terms.

Enter the Due Diligence Process

This is the most dreaded part of the deal process for the seller and intermediary. They have spent a significant amount of time and energy finding the right buyer and negotiating the LOI, and now someone is going to examine the business with a fine-toothed comb. It is the halfway point, and this is where most deals crumble. The seller will be inundated with questions and requests, all without knowing how the process is going from the buyer's point of view. I have included a sample due diligence request (see Appendix C) in order to provide you with a general idea of what may be requested from you.

It is very important to disclose potential issues and less favorable items to the buyer prior to signing the LOI. It is much easier to negotiate the impact of any bad news on the deal price before signing the LOI rather than after signing it.

Most buyers will ask for a period of 60 to 90 days to complete their due diligence. Negotiate this down to no more than 60 days with a due diligence update midway through the process. Having audited financial statements available will make this process go much smoother and quicker. From the buyer's perspective, the quality of information available about your business is critical. If the buyer is not confident that the company's financial statements reflect reality, the deal will die or be subject to a price revision.

Most buyers will hire experienced CPAs and attorneys to go through the financial and legal records. CPAs will look at the quality of historical earnings and make sure that they are sustainable into the future. They will also examine critical areas such as receivable and inventory values, revenue recognition practices, and tax compliance. Typically, they will issue a written report to the buyer. The attorneys will search for potential legal, employee, and environmental issues and examine critical contracts and intellectual property protection.

Make sure that you involve your corporate attorney during this process. You don't have to provide everything the buyer requests. You may not want to turn over your customer list or your secret formulas during this process. Seek the advice of your attorney if the buyer asks for anything that makes you uncomfortable.

If the buyer informs you that items were found in the due diligence process that will impact the terms of the deal, ask for their findings in writing. Take these findings to your advisors to determine their validity and what impact they will have on value.

> **Due Diligence Tip** Have a cooperative tone throughout the process and make it easy for the buyer to obtain the requested item. It raises suspicion if you are belligerent and do not respond properly to a valid request.

Negotiate the Asset Purchase Agreement

The Asset Purchase Agreement (APA) is the definitive agreement that finalizes all terms and conditions related to the sale of your company's assets. It is different from a Stock Purchase Agreement, where the stock is sold including all assets and liabilities. Since a wide majority of deals are asset purchases, we will focus only on the APA. Generally, an APA contains the following items:

- The identification of the specific assets being purchased
- The purchase price
- The amount of cash to be paid at closing
- The details of any seller notes or earn-out
- What assets are excluded from the sale
- What liabilities will be assumed by the purchaser
- The date of closing
- Representations, warranties, and indemnifications
- The allocation of purchase price for tax purposes
- Exhibits that include financial statements

We have discussed most of these items. The exception is the representations, warranties, and indemnifications. It is important that you have an understanding of the purpose of these items in the APA. This is the area where the transaction attorneys earn their fee.

Representations and warranties are statements of fact and assurances made by both the buyer and the seller. Buyers want comprehensive representations and warranties to protect themselves against any problems or unforeseen issues. Sellers want to give as few representations and warranties as they can and limit the financial impact if there is a breach. Indemnification provides one party with a contractual remedy for recovering post-closing monetary damages arising from a breach of a representation, warranty, or any other contract issue.

In the deal that I opened the chapter with, the buyer asserted that there was a breach in the seller's representation about the accuracy of the financial statements. The remedy they sought (indemnification) was the release of the escrow funds to their account and an additional payment by the seller to reduce the price paid. When my client refused these conditions, the buyer sued the seller.

Representations, warranties, and indemnification terms are the focus of a substantial amount of time and energy in negotiations. The only way to avoid this is to agree with all of the buyer's wishes in this area and have a significant portion of your proceeds from the sale held in escrow. However, this approach is not something I would recommend.

As a seller, your goal is to provide reasonable representations and warranties and limit your indemnification exposure. You can place caps on the damage amount, as well as time limits when damages can be claimed. Different areas of exposure may require different time limits. A financial statement representation may expire after one year, but an environmental representation may last much longer.

Land mine Don't minimize the importance of the representations and warranty promises that you make in the APA and understanding the indemnification clause. Don't sign the APA until you are confident that you will not end up in court post-closing.

Close the Deal

This is what you have been waiting for. Sign the APA and get your money! However, most deals do not close upon the signing of the APA, and there can be a small time lag to make sure that the transition from old owner to new owner is smooth. The deal is not closed until you see the funds wired into your account or a check at the closing table. At closing, you will have some deductions from your sale proceeds. Intermediaries receive their fee at closing and other professionals that assisted in the transaction may also insist on being paid at closing. There are no taxes withheld at the closing, and you will need to send what you owe to the IRS based on the recommendations of your tax advisor.

Funds that are held in escrow will be sent to an escrow agent and are released based on the terms in the APA. If buyers make a claim on the escrow funds, they will ask the seller to tell the escrow agent to release the disputed funds to them. At times, there is litigation over the escrow funds. It is important that your APA is very clear about how escrow is released and how disputes are resolved.

The Tax Impact of a Sales Transaction

The saying "don't let the tail wag the dog" applies to the area of taxes on M&A transactions. Taxes are a very important consideration when selling your business but don't let the tax issue drive your decision-making process. Too many business owners fret over taxes rather than growing the value of their business. To retire rich, grow your business. Then when you are ready to sell, hire an M&A tax expert to minimize the impact of taxes on the transaction.

The seller and the buyer have competing interest when it comes to taxes on a deal. Typically, what is good for the seller is not beneficial to the buyer. This is why your tax expert should be brought in early in the process and not at the end of the deal.

In this section, I do not intend to make you a tax expert on M&A transactions. Frankly, this area is too complex for me, and I rely on tax experts in my firm for all M&A transactions. The point I want to make is how important it is to have a tax expert assist you through a transaction. To emphasize this, it's helpful to look at best- and worst-case illustrations.

Each different legal form of business (C corporation, S corporation, LLC, and partnership) has different rules in regards to M&A transactions. Regardless of the legal form of business, the gains on a transaction are either classified as ordinary income or a capital gain. The tax rate difference between ordinary income and capital gains is significant, and there are specific rules from the IRS for what classifies as ordinary income vs. a capital gain.

In order to understand the tax consequences on a sales transaction, I will continue with the example of Fantastic Footballs, Inc. At the end of the last chapter, Charlie's business was worth close to $4 million and we will assume that he receives an offer of $4 million. The two examples that follow demonstrate the difference between a stock sale and an asset sale.

With these calculations, I will assume the highest 2014 tax rates (ignoring the impact of state and local income taxes) and that Fantasy Footballs is a C corporation. For a stock deal, sellers recognize a gain based on the difference between the sales price and their current basis in the stock. Basis is the owner's original investment. If you did not buy your business, the basis of your stock is usually minimal. For this example, Charlie's stock basis is zero. The gain is taxed at the capital gains rate along with the new Medicare surcharge tax on investment income. The federal income tax calculation for the stock transaction is shown here:

Selling Price of Stock	$ 4,000,000
Individual Stock Basis	-
Taxable Gain on Transaction	4,000,000
Capital Gains and Surcharge Tax	23.8%
Federal Taxes on Transaction	$ 952,000

Charlie will have to pay $952,000 in federal income taxes. That's a lot of money. However, it gets worse under an asset deal.

Now let's look at the tax treatment of an asset deal. There is one additional assumption that we need to add. Each asset that a company owns has a tax basis, which is usually the asset's original cost less any depreciation. We will assume that the tax basis of the assets being sold is $2 million. The company receives a check for $4 million and will have a $2 million taxable gain on the transaction. The company has to pay taxes on the difference between the selling price of the assets and the amount on which the assets are recorded on the books for tax purposes (tax basis). After paying the corporate tax on the transaction, business owners then have to pay taxes on the amount that is sent to them personally after the transaction is closed.

In this example, the company owes $680,000 in taxes from reporting a gain on the sale of the assets. The only asset that Fantastic Footballs has now is $3.32 million in cash. Charlie liquidates the company and receives the $3.32 million as a dividend, and he has to pay taxes on that amount at the individual level. Based on the 2013 tax law, Charlie's federal tax rate on this distribution will be 23.8% (dividend rate and Medicare surcharge on investment income). He will owe $790,000 individually on this distribution. The combined corporation and individual tax from the transaction is $1.47 million.

Selling Price of Net Assets	$ 4,000,000
Corporate Basis on Assets Sold	2,000,000
Corporate Gain on Transaction	2,000,000
Corporate Income Tax	34.0%
Federal Taxes on Transaction	680,000
Income Tax on Individual	790,000
Federal Taxes on Transaction	$ 1,470,000

The difference in the income tax bite between an asset deal and the stock deal is huge! It is $518,000. Now this is the worst-case scenario. If Charlie hired a good tax expert, there are legitimate strategies to lower the tax bite of the asset deal.

Tip The basic rule of thumb in M&A transaction is to have as much of the taxable gain classified as a capital gain rather than ordinary income. If the buyer will not allow a stock deal, have your tax advisor show you areas where you can achieve capital gains rates on an asset deal.

Other business entity forms (besides a C corporation) do not have to worry about the double taxation issue (except some S corporations that were once C corporations), but there is still a battle over what is classified as a capital gain and ordinary income.

Both the buyer and the seller will have to include Form 8594 to report the sale to the IRS. On this form, the total selling price of the business is allocated to the various asset classes transferred in the sale. The values entered on the seller's and buyer's copy of Form 8594 must be identical.

My Top Ten Tips in Selling a Business

To end this chapter, here are my top ten tips when it comes to selling your business:

1. Don't wait too long. Exit your business from a position of strength, not weakness. It is important to sell before you become bored with the business, or worse yet, an illness or retirement forces a sale.

2. Have a reasonable expectation on the price that you desire for your business. Since an inflated figure either turns off or slows down potential buyers, rely on a valuation expert to help you arrive at what your company is truly worth. Do not set a price for your business. Instead, have buyers provide you with a price that they are willing to pay. They may surprise you with a price higher than your expectations or true value.

3. Don't let taxes drive your actions but don't neglect their impact.

4. Engage a team of experienced M&A professionals. This is the best way to obtain the highest selling price, minimize your tax burden, and allow you to sleep at night after the deal is closed.

5. Prepare for the sale years in advance. This includes having audited or reviewed statements at your disposal from years back and updating important legal documents.

6. Achieve a higher price through buyer competition. Hire the right intermediary who can create a competitive situation with buyers. The more buyers bidding for your business, the higher price you will obtain.

7. Be flexible. Don't be the kind of seller who wants all cash at the closing, who won't accept any contingent payments, or who insists on a stock transaction.

Chapter 5 | Selling Your Business

8. Disclose potential negative factors early. Make sure that there are no unpleasant surprises for the buyer during the due diligence process. This will save you time and money and avoid killing a deal or renegotiating a price at a lower value.

9. Don't let time drag down the deal. To keep up momentum, work with your advisors to be sure the buyer adheres to a strict time schedule.

10. The line from an old song is true for the M&A process: "You got to know when to hold 'em, know when to fold 'em." If the market or your gut is telling you that this is not the right time to sell after starting the process, pull the plug, reassess, and start the process again when the time is right.

Summary

The most popular exit strategy is the sale of a business. The majority of business owners will eventually sell their business, and it's most likely going to be the largest and most difficult transaction in their lifetime. It's not the time for saving fees by using inexperienced professionals or going through this process alone. The amount received on the sale of your business will impact your financial future.

M&A activity ebbs and flows. It is important that you are ready to enter the market at the right time. The best time to sell is when your business and M&A activity are strong. It is important to have your business in a saleable position in order take advantage of peaks in the market.

Make sure that you have the right professionals on your team. You will need an experienced intermediary, tax professional, and a transaction attorney. Each one has a critical role to play, but always remember that you are the one who is in charge of the process. Do not ignore the impact on income taxes when you sell your business. You can lose 50% of the purchase price to income taxes with an improperly structured deal.

CHAPTER 6

Time for Action

Plans for Cashing Out

The purpose of this book is to provide you, the business owner, with insights in an easy-to-read-in-less-than-four-hours format on how to "cash out" on your most important and valuable asset. I trust you now know how a business is valued, can articulate specific ways to grow that value, and fully understand how a business is sold.

I close this book with some practical tools and concepts to help you start increasing the value of your business and preparing to sell your business at the right time and to the right buyer. But I warn you that there is no Procrustean solution to this process of making your company more valuable and then cashing out.

In Greek mythology, Procrustes was a deceitful character. He enticed weary travelers to stay at his house with a pleasant meal and a night's rest. He would extol his "magical bed" that would be a perfect fit for travelers no matter how tall or short they were. He was right about the bed being a perfect fit. However, the travelers were sorry that they slept on his magical bed. If they were too long for the bed, he chopped their feet off. And if they were too short for the bed, he would stretch the guests until they were the same length as the bed. It was truly a one-size-fits-all bed.

A *Procrustean solution* is the practice of tailoring complex issues into a one-size-fits-all plan. There are consultants, advisors, and books that will either sell you on their preconceived notion of what your exit strategy should be or use a one-size-fits-all packaged solution. But Procrustean solutions for increasing the value of your business and selling your business are doomed to fail, because they will do violence to the organic reality of your particular business and your particular needs.

In the absence of an out-of-the-box solution, you may feel a little overwhelmed at this point about how to start the process of improving your business value and selecting the right buyer. I am going to close this book with some tips to prime the pump and get you started.

Critical Items to Your Plan's Success

Too many strategic and growth plans are sitting in the top drawer of the business owner's desk collecting dust. Many of these plans have a lot of nice-looking color graphs and slick photos that would impress anyone. The owner spent significant time and money developing the plan. But it is completely worthless while it is gathering dust. How do you make sure all of your hard work and money spent on the planning process will be worth the effort? I believe that there are three critical concepts that you need to embrace in order to make your plan a success.

The first concept is *setting the right tone from the top*. You need to communicate that the execution of the plan is very important to you and that you are allocating a significant amount of time and resources to accomplish the plan. Your employees will see that you are serious about this and know that they will be held accountable for their contribution to the plan. If it is not known to be important to you, it will not be important to others.

The second concept is *selecting the right people for your team*. It can be a very lonely position being a business owner, and some owners slip into silo-thinking and are not open to outside ideas. We all have blind spots and self-serving biases that lead us down the wrong path. It is important that you have members of your team (advisors and employees) who can provide you with candor and are not afraid to challenge you. You want team members who can push and exhort each other to obtain the best result.

The third concept is *making sure that your plan is achievable and tailored to your situation and culture*. The reason why so many plans collect dust is because they are either too ambitious or too theoretical. I remember seeing a plan that had over 100 goals and action items with some impressive words that I did not understand. The plan did not accomplish much. The employees knew from Day One that those goals and action items could not be accomplished. Make sure that all those involved understand what is being asked of them and that they believe that they can perform their assigned tasks in the time frame requested.

Plans to Grow Your Value

There is not much published about how to develop a specific plan to grow the value of your business investment. You may be able to look at one of the many strategic planning books to assist you in creating a plan to grow the value of your business. You need to tailor that advice to focus on growing your business value and try not to get too bogged down by the process or the terminology that is used in these books. Many authors make the strategic planning process too complex. In my opinion, a simple straightforward plan works the best.

The following are the steps that I suggest you take in developing and executing a plan to grow the value of your business:

1. Know the current value of your business.
2. Set a growth goal for your business value.
3. Identify ways you can increase the value of your business from the following valuation drivers:
    - Increasing your sustainable future cash flow
    - Lowering your business risks
    - Increasing your growth prospects
4. Select goals that are attainable and measurable and then develop strategies and action plans to achieve those goals.
5. Assign responsibilities and hold people accountable.
6. Have quarterly meetings to monitor the progress.
7. Reassess when necessary.

This book has discussed at length the importance of having a business valuation and how it is not possible to start your growth plan without a realistic view of what your business is worth. Once you have determined the value, it is important to set a growth goal. You may set an annual percentage increase-in-value goal or an amount that you want your business to be worth at the end of a certain time period. Whatever method you choose, it is important to have a target set for your future business value.

Once you know the value of your business and set a target for its future value, the next step is to identify ways to increase the value of your business. The approach that I like best is to spend a day with the business owner and key employees away from their facility and discuss the critical areas that are impacting the value of the business. I rank the items in the order of biggest impact on value, and I have the management team rank the items in the order of those they feel they can influence the most. This exercise results in a consensus on what items the team should focus on during the next months and years to increase the value of the business.

The next step is to select two to four specific goals that the management team will concentrate on to make the business more valuable. I like to make sure that there is a consensus on the selected goals and that these goals can be achieved and progress measured. Having a plan and stated goals is great, but it is actually the easy part. It is like reading a book about fitness, buying the gym membership, and hiring the personal trainer. Without showing up and working out, you will not reach your physical goals. The same goes for your plan to grow the value of your business. The right execution plan is critical.

For each goal, select a champion who will be responsible for the achievement of that goal. This person's job is to develop the right strategies and actions to accomplish the goal. You need to have in place the right people who have the time and resources to get the job done. To help ensure the plan continues on course, hold quarterly meetings that focus only on the progress being made in increasing the value of the business. These meetings offer an opportunity to remind everyone what the plan entails and how each person contributes to the success of the plan.

There will be a time when it becomes evident that a particular goal or champion for that goal needs to be changed. Reassess and step back. Also, look at your value growth plan on an annual basis or when a major event takes place. Your plan is a living, fluid document, and reassessing it provides you with the opportunity to change the goal, tactics, or personnel if the situation warrants.

Tip Have your quarterly meetings to discuss the progress of your plan at an offsite location. Don't allow your team to be distracted by the day-to-day issues when discussing the plan to grow the value of your business.

Plans for Cashing Out

Maybe the timing of the sale of your business and who the ultimate buyer will be is clear to you. If so, have you prepared an analysis of what your after-tax proceeds will be from your current strategy? Does this amount, along with your other assets, provide you with the retirement you desire? This analysis will provide you with a litmus test of how close you are to achieving your financial goals under your current strategy. After seeing how your plans play out on paper, you may choose a different strategy or become more focused on increasing the value of your business.

What if you don't know who the ultimate buyer will be and when you will sell your business? How can you make a decision in this important area? What can you do today to start the process that allows you to exit your business on your terms?

Don't look around for a one-size-fits-all Procrustean solution that will dictate your best strategy. It will take time and hard work to make sure you have the right plan. If you take the following steps during the next 12 to 18 months, you will be closer to having a well-defined strategy for "cashing out" of your business:

- Study the various types of buyers (see Chapter 5) and understand the advantages and disadvantages of each buyer as they apply to your situation.
- Estimate the net after-tax proceeds that will you will obtain from each type of buyer. Each type of buyer will provide you with a different outcome.
- Spend time reflecting on how your decision will impact the future of your family and the employees of your company.
- Think about the future and whether your company will become more or less valuable? Are you better off "cashing out" sooner or later?
- Develop plans on how you will spend your time once you leave your business. Are they attractive to you?

You have spent a lot of blood, sweat, and tears in starting and operating your business. It is not an easy process of turning over the keys of your baby to someone else.

Discuss your thoughts about the timing of the sale of your business and the type of buyer you would like to pursue with your spouse, kids, and trusted advisors. Each buyer type requires a different strategy and focus. It is never too early to work on your selling strategy and making your company more attractive to the ultimate buyer.

Summary

Your business will not become more attractive and more valuable to the ultimate buyer without significant planning and focused attention on accomplishing your plan. The business owner has to be very proactive in growing the value of the business, and it is important to have specific goals and action plans. Don't be afraid to change your goals and strategies as your plan progresses and you obtain more visibility. By setting a course of action, you will achieve greater riches than by not putting a plan into place.

APPENDIX A

Sample Engagement Letter

January 30, 2015

Charlie Sample

Chairman & CEO

Fantastic Footballs, Inc.

Sample, Ohio 99999

Dear Mr. Sample:

We appreciate the opportunity to provide you our valuation services. This letter outlines our understanding of the terms and objectives of the engagement.

We will perform a valuation of your common stock interest in Fantastic Footballs, Inc. for business and estate planning purposes. Our valuation will include a per share value on both a controlling and noncontrolling interest. The date of the valuation will be as of December 31, 2014.

Appendix A | Sample Engagement Letter

We will provide you with two opinions of value. The standards of value that will be used in this engagement are "fair market value" and "investment value." The term "fair market value" is defined as follows:

> *The price at which the property would change hands between a willing buyer and a willing seller, neither being under a compulsion to buy or sell and both having reasonable knowledge of relevant facts.*

The term "investment value" is defined as follows:

> *The price to a specific buyer or investor often based on perceived synergies when the business is combined with another business.*

We plan to start the engagement when your staff is available to provide us with the requested information, and unless unforeseen problems are encountered, we will provide you with a report draft within 45 days of receiving all requested documents.

In performing our valuation, we will be relying upon the accuracy and reliability of the operations' historical financial statements, forecasts of future operations, or other financial data. We will not audit, compile, or review those financial statements, forecasts, or financial data and will not express an opinion or any form of assurance on them. Our engagement cannot be relied upon to disclose errors, irregularities, or illegal acts, including fraud or defalcations, that may exist. At the conclusion of the engagement, we will ask you or any authorized official of the Company to sign a representation letter on the accuracy and reliability of the financial information used in the engagement.

We will document the results of the engagement in a full valuation report. We understand our valuation conclusion will serve as a basis for the stated purpose in this letter, and the distribution of the report is restricted to this purpose and will not be used for any other purpose or by any unintended user, or with respect to any other date. We have no responsibility to update our valuation report for events and circumstances that occur after the date of its issuance. If for any reason we are unable to complete the valuation engagement, we will not issue a report as a result of the engagement.

Our method of valuation follows the guidelines set forth by the Internal Revenue Service (IRS) in its Revenue Ruling 59-60, as well as conforming to the appraisal standards promulgated by the American Society of Appraisers and the American Institute of Certified Public Accountants.

The fee for our valuation service and the final report will be $ XXXX. We will send you progress invoices on a monthly basis. All invoices will be due and payable upon receipt. Our fee is for the valuation report and does not include any other services that may be required to issue our report (e.g. equipment appraisal). We will require a retainer of $XXXX before we proceed with this engagement. All invoices will be due and payable upon receipt. A service charge of 1½% per month (18% per annum) will be added to past due balances. We will not issue the final report until the balance is paid in full. We appreciate this opportunity to be of service to you and look forward to working with you on this important engagement. If you agree with the foregoing terms, please sign the copy of this letter in the space provided below and return a signed copy back to us.

Sincerely,

Tim McDaniel, CPA/ABV, ASA, CBA

Director of Valuation & Succession Planning Services

_____

Signature

_____

Date

APPENDIX B

Sample Due Diligence Request

The following is a list of documents and other information that a buyer may request during the due diligence process. Each buyer and transaction is unique, and what is requested will differ among buyers. This sample is only intended to provide you with a general idea of items that may be requested from you in an M&A transaction and should not be considered as a complete list.

Organization and Records

- A staff organization chart, listing all employees with titles and grade levels and any open positions.
- Biographies and resumes for all company executives.
- Employee Handbook (including new employee orientation documents). Provide the human resources policies relating to sexual harassment, background investigations, and drug testing.
- Copy of articles or certificate of incorporation and any amendments.
- Copy of by-laws or code of regulations and any amendments.

- Copy of all resolutions and minutes of board of director meetings.
- List of states where the company conducts business and a list of states where the company has obtained a Certificate of Good Standing.
- List of stockholders and their stock ownership (include stock options or similar rights, if applicable).
- All stockholders' agreements and other agreements relating to transfer restrictions or voting rights with respect to any equity securities.
- Any agreements relating to partnerships or a joint venture that the company is part of.
- Copies of the company's documentation retention or destruction policy.

Financial Statements and Records

General

- Annual financial statements from an outside accountant for the past five years.
- Internal financial statements for the most recent year to date and a comparison statement for the similar period of the prior year.
- Auditor's review letters and management letters for the last five years.
- Operating budgets and capital expenditure budgets for the most recent year, the current year, and any future periods.
- Description of any changes in accounting methods during the past five years.

Assets

- List of all bank accounts (including name of bank, owner of the account, the account number, current balance, and authorized signatories).
- Accounts receivable aging report as of the most recent month end.

- List of accounts in dispute or collection proceedings.
- Total of credit balances owed to customers as of latest month end.
- Fixed-asset detail listing with depreciation schedules as of the latest fiscal year.
- List of actual capital expenditures for past three years and year to date.
- List of all real property used by the business by location, including street address, county, and state. Indicate whether such real property is owned or leased.
- Inventory aging report as of the most recent month end. Identify all inventories that are greater than 180 days.
- UCC searches for all assets, together with a description of all liens or security interests.
- Schedule and copies of all leases (both capital and operating) and installment purchase contracts with annual minimum commitments in excess of $10,000.
- All material deeds, leases (for real estate or personal property), or options to purchase personal property.
- All reports, surveys, studies (including environmental reports), and independent appraisals of all land or other property that is either owned or leased by the company.

Liabilities

- Schedule of all outstanding long-term and short-term debt (other than normal trade payables) including payee, origination date, due date, interest rate, monthly payment, security and current balance.
- All loan agreements and credit instruments, debt instruments, indentures, security agreements, mortgages, promissory notes, guarantees and letters of credit, and other similar instruments evidencing borrowings and any related security documents.
- All other material agreements with creditors, including any documentation with respect to representations given to creditors in connection with obtaining credit.
- List of all mortgages, liens, and security interests in properties belonging to the company.

- All agreements or other documents relating to any loans or advances to, or investments in, other entities.
- Computation demonstrating compliance with financial covenants in existing financing documents.
- List of all obligations that are not listed on the balance sheet in excess of $10,000.

Salaries and Benefits

- List of all employees, together with job descriptions, actual compensation for prior year, and targeted compensation for current year.
- Written description of compensation formula (i.e., salary plus incentive compensation plus anything else), related pay dates, and the pay periods covered.
- Year-to-date and prior-year quarterly payroll tax returns (Form 941).
- IRS Form 5500 for prior three years. Include the summary annual reports for qualified pension or 401(k) plans, profit sharing plans, and health & welfare plans.
- Current plan documents and all amendments since inception of plan(s) pertaining to qualified pension/401(k) and profit sharing plans, including summary plan descriptions and a summary of material modifications.
- Current plan documents and all amendments for any deferred-compensation plans.
- Most recent favorable determination letter and copy of IRS Form 5300 and supporting documents.
- Copy of the investment management agreement and plan administration agreement with record keeper, including latest invoice for services.
- Notices from Department of Labor and IRS since inception of plan, including any notices concerning Form 5500 reporting deficiencies related to late filings and plan audit matters.
- Plan investment records for most recent plan year pertaining to qualified pension and profit sharing plans.

- Contribution history for prior three years pertaining to qualified pension and profit sharing plans.
- Copies of discrimination test results for prior three years pertaining to all retirement plans and cafeteria plans.
- Current plan documents, amendments, and summary plan descriptions pertaining to health care plan.
- Copies of insurance contracts and service agreements, including most recent invoices, pertaining to health care plan.
- A summary of the vacation policy.
- A summary of other paid time-off policies (sickness, holidays, and jury duty).
- List of vacation hours accrued but not yet taken for each employee as of the most recent year end.
- Copies of workers' compensation filings and a list of all claims that have occurred during the past five years.

Tax-related Items

- Copies of federal, state, and local tax returns for the past five years.
- Copies of any settlement documents, correspondence from taxing authorities, currently pending tax disputes, proceedings, or issues for the preceding five years.
- Information regarding extension of statutes, if applicable.
- Any private letter rulings or other correspondence about specific tax issues with the IRS.
- Status and list of any audits in progress (federal, state, and local).
- Copies of any special tax elections filed by the company.
- Copies of sales-and-use tax returns for last three years.
- Copies of property tax returns for last three years.
- Description of any tax abatement or incentive agreements.

Employee Matters

- Copies of all contracts or commitments for the employment of any employee, independent contractor, consultant, or advisor.

- Copies of all agreements, contracts, or commitments relating to any bonus, deferred compensation, pension, profit sharing, stock option, employee stock purchase, retirement, medical life insurance, disability, or other employee benefit plan.

- Copies of covenants not to compete and secrecy agreements with any employee or former employee, which are still valid.

- Description of past labor disputes, requests for arbitration, strikes and other labor disruptions, complaints, or other claims of unfair labor practices and material grievance proceedings.

- Copy of the current union agreement and status of current negotiations.

- Description of any material, oral agreements, or understandings with employees.

- Statement of the licensure status of all professional employees.

Market and Sales Overview

- Description of the size of the market and how the market is segmented.

- Any forecast of the market's projected growth.

- Detailed summary of the profitability by product, customer, and segment.

- List of new products in the pipeline and estimates of the remaining time and expense required to launch each new product.

- List of sales to the top ten customers for the past three years and a description of how long the company had sales relationships with the top ten customers.

- Description of the sales process through the Internet.

- Description of any customer contracts that are coming up for renewal and any likely changes to the key terms of those agreements.
- Details of history of complaints from customers and a list of any customers who have indicated that they will no longer be a customer in the future.
- Results of any customer satisfaction surveys.

Material Contracts and Other Documents

- List of all vendors or suppliers.
- List of purchases by vendor for the ten largest vendors for the latest two fiscal years and year to date.
- Web site hosting and connectivity agreements.
- Copies of all contracts and agreements for the future purchase of materials, supplies, equipment, or services that calls for or could result in payments of more than $10,000.
- Copies of all current and future contracts and agreements for the sale of products or services that exceed $10,000.
- Copies of noncompete or similar agreements which restrict or limit the company or its representatives from engaging in any type of business.
- Copies of any contracts, instruments, judgments, or decrees that might reasonably be expected to adversely affect the business practices, operations, or condition of the company or any property.
- Description of any material oral agreements or understandings.
- Copies of all documents and agreements evidencing other material financing arrangements including sale-and-leaseback arrangements and installment purchases.
- Copies of all secrecy, confidentiality, and nondisclosure agreements to which the company is a party.
- Copies of all contracts or agreements to which directors, officers, or shareholders of the company (or members of their families) are parties.

- Copies of all material permits, licenses, or governmental consents required to conduct the business of the company as it is now conducted.
- Copies of all reports filed and significant correspondence with any state or federal regulatory agency during the past three years.
- Description of the company's use of and policies regarding independent contractors and the amount of payment in current and prior year.

Legal and Litigation Matters

- Schedule of all litigation, administrative, regulatory, or judicial proceedings or governmental investigations pending or threatened by or against the company, including the name of the case, nature of the suit, amount sought in the complaint, name and location of the court in which the case is pending, and estimated amount of potential judgment.
- Schedule and summary of all litigation or other proceedings settled or otherwise resolved within the past five years.
- Documentation regarding any litigation or other proceeding involving any officer or director of the company concerning bankruptcy, crimes, securities, or business practices.
- Copies of all consent decrees, judgments, other decrees or orders, settlement agreements, and other agreements to which the company is a party.
- Copies of all notices or demand letters regarding or relating to any material claims by or against the company with respect to which no litigation has yet been filed.
- Copies of all notices, citations, and other communications received in the past three years from any governmental agency filed in regards to the company in its business operations, or compliance with any applicable governmental regulations.
- Copies of insurance company loss runs for all coverages, including auto liability, and general and professional liability coverage for the past five years.

- Copies of any open charges of discrimination, complaints, or related litigation, or any such cases that have been closed within the past five years.
- Schedule of warranty claims.
- Copy of all legal invoices for the past three years.

Intellectual Property

- List of all patents, patent applications, trademarks, service marks, trade names, copyrights, know-how, and trade secrets owned or used by the company with the status of each.
- Itemized list of all potential patents that have not been applied for.
- All unregistered trademarks and service marks used by the organization.
- All copyright registrations.
- Copies of all material license agreements pertaining to software or other intangible assets.
- Product documentation and manuals for the company's software, databases, and networks (or other description of primary capabilities).
- Copies of all licenses of intellectual property in which the company is the licensor or licensee.
- List of the company's Internet sites and newsgroups.
- Copies of any royalty agreements (whether the company pays or receives the royalty).
- Summary of research-and-development expenditures over the last five years.

Miscellaneous

- Description of any earn-outs or contingent consideration related to any completed acquisitions.
- Schedule of all transactions with related parties (or their families) and future obligations.
- List of all outside consultants and the services performed during the past five years. Copies of any reports received from any consultants, including environmental, human resources, and marketing.
- Description of the backup systems in place with offsite storage, both for the corporate-level databases and for individual computers.
- Any other document or information that is significant with respect to the business of the company.

APPENDIX

C

AICPA Statement on Standards for Valuation Services No. 1

Excerpts for Valuation Reports and Glossary of Valuation Terms[*]

The Valuation Report

47. A valuation report is a written or oral communication to the client containing the conclusion of value or the calculated value of the subject interest. Reports issued for purposes of certain controversy proceedings are exempt from this reporting standard (paragraph 50).

---

[*]Copyright © 2007, American Institute of CPAs. All rights reserved. Used with permission. www.aicpa.org/InterestAreas/ForensicAndValuation/Resources/Standards/DownloadableDocuments/SSVS_Full_Version.pdf

48. The three types of written reports that a valuation analyst may use to communicate the results of an engagement to estimate value are: for a valuation engagement, a detailed report or a summary report; and for a calculation engagement, a calculation report.

For a Valuation Engagement

a. *Detailed Report*: This report may be used only to communicate the results of a valuation engagement (conclusion of value); it should not be used to communicate the results of a calculation engagement (calculated value) (paragraph 51).

b. *Summary Report*: This report may be used only to communicate the results of a valuation engagement (conclusion of value); it should not be used to communicate the results of a calculation engagement (calculated value) (paragraph 71).

For a valuation engagement, the determination of whether to prepare a detailed report or a summary report is based on the level of reporting detail agreed to by the valuation analyst and the client.

49. The valuation analyst should indicate in the valuation report the restrictions on the use of the report (which may include restrictions on the users of the report, the uses of the report by such users, or both) (paragraph 65(d)).

Detailed Report

...

51. The *detailed report* is structured to provide sufficient information to permit intended users to understand the data, reasoning, and analyses underlying the valuation analyst's conclusion of value. A detailed report should include, as applicable, the following sections titled using wording similar in content to that shown:

- Letter of transmittal
- Table of contents
- Introduction
- Sources of information
- Analysis of the subject entity and related nonfinancial information
- Financial statement/information analysis

- Valuation approaches and methods considered
- Valuation approaches and methods used
- Valuation adjustments
- Nonoperating assets, nonoperating liabilities, and excess or deficient operating assets (if any)
- Representation of the valuation analyst
- Reconciliation of estimates and conclusion of value
- Qualifications of the valuation analyst
- Appendices and exhibits

The above listed report sections and the detailed information within the sections described in the following paragraphs 52–77 may be positioned in the body of the report or elsewhere in the report at the discretion of the valuation analyst.

Introduction

52. This section should provide an overall description of the valuation engagement. The information in the section should be sufficient to enable the intended user of the report to understand the nature and scope of the valuation engagement, as well as the work performed. The introduction section may include, among other things, the following information:

   a. Identity of the client
   b. Purpose and intended use of the valuation
   c. Intended users of the valuation
   d. Identity of the subject entity
   e. Description of the subject interest
   f. Whether the business interest has ownership control characteristics and its degree of marketability
   g. Valuation date
   h. Report date
   i. Type of report issued (namely, a detailed report) (paragraph 51)
   j. Applicable premise of value
   k. Applicable standard of value

l. Assumptions and limiting conditions (alternatively, these often appear in an appendix) (paragraph 18)

m. Any restrictions or limitations in the scope of work or data available for analysis (paragraph 19)

n. Any hypothetical conditions used in the valuation engagement, including the basis for their use (paragraph 22)

o. If the work of a specialist was used in the valuation engagement, a description of how the specialist's work was relied upon (paragraph 20)

p. Disclosure of subsequent events in certain circumstances (paragraph 43)

q. Any application of the jurisdictional exception (paragraph 10)

r. Any additional information the valuation analyst deems useful to enable the user(s) of the report to understand the work performed

If the above items are not included in the introduction, they should be included elsewhere in the valuation report.

Summary Report

...

71. A summary report is structured to provide an abridged version of the information that would be provided in a detailed report, and therefore, need not contain the same level of detail as a detailed report. However, a summary report should, at a minimum, include the following:

a. Identity of the client

b. Purpose and intended use of the valuation

c. Intended users of the valuation

d. Identity of the subject entity

e. Description of the subject interest

f. The business interest's ownership control characteristics, if any, and its degree of marketability

g. Valuation date
h. Valuation report date
i. Type of report issued (namely, a summary report) (paragraph 48)
j. Applicable premise of value
k. Applicable standard of value
l. Sources of information used in the valuation engagement
m. Assumptions and limiting conditions of the valuation engagement (paragraph 18)
n. The scope of work or data available for analysis including any restrictions or limitations (paragraph 19)
o. Any hypothetical conditions used in the valuation engagement, including the basis for their use (paragraph 22)
p. If the work of a specialist was used in the valuation (paragraph 20), a description of how the specialist's work was used, and the level of responsibility, if any, the valuation analyst is assuming for the specialist's work
q. The valuation approaches and methods used
r. Disclosure of subsequent events in certain circumstances (paragraph 43)
s. Any application of the jurisdictional exception (paragraph 10)
t. Representation of the valuation analyst (paragraph 65)
u. The report is signed in the name of the valuation analyst or the valuation analyst's firm
v. A section summarizing the reconciliation of the estimates and the conclusion of value as discussed in paragraphs 68 and 69

...

APPENDIX B: International Glossary of Business Valuation Terms†

To enhance and sustain the quality of business valuations for the benefit of the profession and its clientele, the below identified societies and organizations have adopted the definitions for the terms included in this glossary.

The performance of business valuation services requires a high degree of skill and imposes upon the valuation professional a duty to communicate the valuation process and conclusion in a manner that is clear and not misleading. This duty is advanced through the use of terms whose meanings are clearly established and consistently applied throughout the profession.

If, in the opinion of the business valuation professional, one or more of these terms needs to be used in a manner which materially departs from the enclosed definitions, it is recommended that the term be defined as used within that valuation engagement.

This glossary has been developed to provide guidance to business valuation practitioners by further memorializing the body of knowledge that constitutes the competent and careful determination of value and, more particularly, the communication of how that value was determined.

Departure from this glossary is not intended to provide a basis for civil liability and should not be presumed to create evidence that any duty has been breached.

American Institute of Certified Public Accountants

American Society of Appraisers

Canadian Institute of Chartered Business Valuators

National Association of Certified Valuation Analysts

The Institute of Business Appraisers

Adjusted Book Value Method—a method within the asset approach whereby all assets and liabilities (including off-balance sheet, intangible, and contingent) are adjusted to their fair market values. {NOTE: In Canada on a going concern basis}

---

†Reproduced verbatim from the International Glossary of Business Valuation Terms (the Glossary), which appears at http://bvfls.aicpa.org/Resources/Business+Valuation/ Tools+and+ Aids/Definitions+and+Terms/International+ Glossary+of+Business+Valuation+Terms.htm. Note that the phrase, "we discourage the use of this term," that appears herein is also reproduced verbatim.

Arbitrage Pricing Theory—a multivariate model for estimating the cost of equity capital, which incorporates several systematic risk factors.

Asset (Asset-Based) Approach—a general way of determining a value indication of a business, business ownership interest, or security using one or more methods based on the value of the assets net of liabilities.

Beta—a measure of systematic risk of a stock; the tendency of a stock's price to correlate with changes in a specific index.

Blockage Discount—an amount or percentage deducted from the current market price of a publicly traded stock to reflect the decrease in the per share value of a block of stock that is of a size that could not be sold in a reasonable period of time given normal trading volume.

Book Value—see **Net Book Value**.

Business—see **Business Enterprise**.

Business Enterprise—a commercial, industrial, service, or investment entity (or a combination thereof) pursuing an economic activity.

Business Risk—the degree of uncertainty of realizing expected future returns of the business resulting from factors other than financial leverage. See **Financial Risk**.

Business Valuation—the act or process of determining the value of a business enterprise or ownership interest therein.

Capital Asset Pricing Model (CAPM)—a model in which the cost of capital for any stock or portfolio of stocks equals a risk-free rate plus a risk premium that is proportionate to the systematic risk of the stock or portfolio.

Capitalization—a conversion of a single period of economic benefits into value.

Capitalization Factor—any multiple or divisor used to convert anticipated economic benefits of a single period into value.

Capitalization of Earnings Method—a method within the income approach whereby economic benefits for a representative single period are converted to value through division by a capitalization rate.

Capitalization Rate—any divisor (usually expressed as a percentage) used to convert anticipated economic benefits of a single period into value.

Capital Structure—the composition of the invested capital of a business enterprise; the mix of debt and equity financing.

Cash Flow—cash that is generated over a period of time by an asset, group of assets, or business enterprise. It may be used in a general sense to encompass various levels of specifically defined cash flows. When the term is used, it should be supplemented by a qualifier (for example, "discretionary" or "operating") and a specific definition in the given valuation context.

Common Size Statements—financial statements in which each line is expressed as a percentage of the total. On the balance sheet, each line item is shown as a percentage of total assets, and on the income statement, each item is expressed as a percentage of sales.

Control—the power to direct the management and policies of a business enterprise.

Control Premium—an amount or a percentage by which the pro rata value of a controlling interest exceeds the pro rata value of a noncontrolling interest in a business enterprise to reflect the power of control.

Cost Approach—a general way of determining a value indication of an individual asset by quantifying the amount of money required to replace the future service capability of that asset.

Cost of Capital—the expected rate of return that the market requires in order to attract funds to a particular investment.

Debt-Free—*we discourage the use of this term.* See **Invested Capital**.

Discount for Lack of Control—an amount or percentage deducted from the pro rata share of value of 100% of an equity interest in a business to reflect the absence of some or all of the powers of control.

Discount for Lack of Marketability—an amount or percentage deducted from the value of an ownership interest to reflect the relative absence of marketability.

Discount for Lack of Voting Rights—an amount or percentage deducted from the per share value of a minority interest voting share to reflect the absence of voting rights.

Discount Rate—a rate of return used to convert a future monetary sum into present value.

Discounted Cash Flow Method—a method within the income approach whereby the present value of future expected net cash flows is calculated using a discount rate.

Discounted Future Earnings Method—a method within the income approach whereby the present value of future expected economic benefits is calculated using a discount rate.

Economic Benefits—inflows such as revenues, net income, net cash flows, etc.

Economic Life—the period of time over which property may generate economic benefits.

Effective Date—see **Valuation Date**.

Enterprise—see **Business Enterprise**.

Equity—the owner's interest in property after deduction of all liabilities.

Equity Net Cash Flows—those cash flows available to pay out to equity holders (in the form of dividends) after funding operations of the business enterprise, making necessary capital investments, and increasing or decreasing debt financing.

Equity Risk Premium—a rate of return added to a risk-free rate to reflect the additional risk of equity instruments over risk free instruments (a component of the cost of equity capital or equity discount rate).

Excess Earnings—that amount of anticipated economic benefits that exceeds an appropriate rate of return on the value of a selected asset base (often net tangible assets) used to generate those anticipated economic benefits.

Excess Earnings Method—a specific way of determining a value indication of a business, business ownership interest, or security determined as the sum of a) the value of the assets derived by capitalizing excess earnings and b) the value of the selected asset base. Also frequently used to value intangible assets. See **Excess Earnings**.

Fair Market Value—the price, expressed in terms of cash equivalents, at which property would change hands between a hypothetical willing and able buyer and a hypothetical willing and able seller, acting at arm's length in an open and unrestricted market, when neither is under compulsion to buy or sell and when both have reasonable knowledge of the relevant facts. {NOTE: In Canada, the term "price" should be replaced with the term "highest price".}

Fairness Opinion—an opinion as to whether or not the consideration in a transaction is fair from a financial point of view.

Financial Risk—the degree of uncertainty of realizing expected future returns of the business resulting from financial leverage. See **Business Risk**.

Forced Liquidation Value—liquidation value, at which the asset or assets are sold as quickly as possible, such as at an auction.

Free Cash Flow—we discourage the use of this term. See **Net Cash Flow**.

Going Concern—an ongoing operating business enterprise.

Going Concern Value—the value of a business enterprise that is expected to continue to operate into the future. The intangible elements of Going Concern Value result from factors such as having a trained work force, an operational plant, and the necessary licenses, systems, and procedures in place.

Goodwill—that intangible asset arising as a result of name, reputation, customer loyalty, location, products, and similar factors not separately identified.

Goodwill Value—the value attributable to goodwill.

Guideline Public Company Method—a method within the market approach whereby market multiples are derived from market prices of stocks of companies that are engaged in the same or similar lines of business and that are actively traded on a free and open market.

Income (Income-Based) Approach—a general way of determining a value indication of a business, business ownership interest, security, or intangible asset using one or more methods that convert anticipated economic benefits into a present single amount.

Intangible Assets—nonphysical assets such as franchises, trade-marks, patents, copyrights, goodwill, equities, mineral rights, securities, and contracts (as distinguished from physical assets) that grant rights and privileges and have value for the owner.

Internal Rate of Return—a discount rate at which the present value of the future cash flows of the investment equals the cost of the investment.

Intrinsic Value—the value that an investor considers, on the basis of an evaluation or available facts, to be the "true" or "real" value that will become the market value when other investors reach the same conclusion. When the term applies to options, it is the difference between the exercise price and strike price of an option and the market value of the underlying security.

Invested Capital—the sum of equity and debt in a business enterprise. Debt is typically (a) all interest-bearing debt or (b) long-term, interest-bearing debt. When the term is used, it should be supplemented by a specific definition in the given valuation context.

Invested Capital Net Cash Flows—those cash flows available to pay out to equity holders (in the form of dividends) and debt investors (in the form of principal and interest) after funding operations of the business enterprise and making necessary capital investments.

Investment Risk—the degree of uncertainty as to the realization of expected returns.

Investment Value—the value to a particular investor based on individual investment requirements and expectations. {NOTE: In Canada, the term used is "Value to the Owner".}

Key Person Discount—an amount or percentage deducted from the value of an ownership interest to reflect the reduction in value resulting from the actual or potential loss of a key person in a business enterprise.

Levered Beta—the beta reflecting a capital structure that includes debt.

Limited Appraisal—the act or process of determining the value of a business, business ownership interest, security, or intangible asset with limitations in analyses, procedures, or scope.

Liquidity—the ability to quickly convert property to cash or pay a liability.

Liquidation Value—the net amount that would be realized if the business is terminated and the assets are sold piecemeal. Liquidation can be either "orderly" or "forced."

Majority Control—the degree of control provided by a majority position.

Majority Interest—an ownership interest greater than 50% of the voting interest in a business enterprise.

Market (Market-Based) Approach—a general way of determining a value indication of a business, business ownership interest, security, or intangible asset by using one or more methods that compare the subject to similar businesses, business ownership interests, securities, or intangible assets that have been sold.

Market Capitalization of Equity—the share price of a publicly traded stock multiplied by the number of shares outstanding.

Market Capitalization of Invested Capital—the market capitalization of equity plus the market value of the debt component of invested capital.

Market Multiple—the market value of a company's stock or invested capital divided by a company measure (such as economic benefits, number of customers).

Marketability—the ability to quickly convert property to cash at minimal cost.

Marketability Discount—see **Discount for Lack of Marketability**.

Merger and Acquisition Method—a method within the market approach whereby pricing multiples are derived from transactions of significant interests in companies engaged in the same or similar lines of business.

Mid-Year Discounting—a convention used in the Discounted Future Earnings Method that reflects economic benefits being generated at mid-year, approximating the effect of economic benefits being generated evenly throughout the year.

Minority Discount—a discount for lack of control applicable to a minority interest.

Minority Interest—an ownership interest less than 50% of the voting interest in a business enterprise.

Multiple—the inverse of the capitalization rate.

Net Book Value—with respect to a business enterprise, the difference between total assets (net of accumulated depreciation, depletion, and amortization) and total liabilities as they appear on the balance sheet (synonymous with Shareholder's Equity). With respect to a specific asset, the capitalized cost less accumulated amortization or depreciation as it appears on the books of account of the business enterprise.

Net Cash Flows—when the term is used, it should be supplemented by a qualifier. See **Equity Net Cash Flows** and **Invested Capital Net Cash Flows**.

Net Present Value—the value, as of a specified date, of future cash inflows less all cash outflows (including the cost of investment) calculated using an appropriate discount rate.

Net Tangible Asset Value—the value of the business enterprise's tangible assets (excluding excess assets and nonoperating assets) minus the value of its liabilities.

Nonoperating Assets—assets not necessary to ongoing operations of the business enterprise. {NOTE: In Canada, the term used is "Redundant Assets".}

Normalized Earnings—economic benefits adjusted for nonrecurring, noneconomic, or other unusual items to eliminate anomalies and/or facilitate comparisons.

Normalized Financial Statements—financial statements adjusted for nonoperating assets and liabilities and/or for nonrecurring, noneconomic, or other unusual items to eliminate anomalies and/or facilitate comparisons.

Orderly Liquidation Value—liquidation value at which the asset or assets are sold over a reasonable period of time to maximize proceeds received.

Premise of Value—an assumption regarding the most likely set of transactional circumstances that may be applicable to the subject valuation; for example, going concern, liquidation.

Present Value—the value, as of a specified date, of future economic benefits and/or proceeds from sale, calculated using an appropriate discount rate.

Portfolio Discount—an amount or percentage deducted from the value of a business enterprise to reflect the fact that it owns dissimilar operations or assets that do not fit well together.

Price/Earnings Multiple—the price of a share of stock divided by its earnings per share.

Rate of Return—an amount of income (loss) and/or change in value realized or anticipated on an investment, expressed as a percentage of that investment.

Redundant Assets—see **Nonoperating Assets**.

Report Date—the date conclusions are transmitted to the client.

Replacement Cost New—the current cost of a similar new property having the nearest equivalent utility to the property being valued.

Reproduction Cost New—the current cost of an identical new property.

Required Rate of Return—the minimum rate of return acceptable by investors before they will commit money to an investment at a given level of risk.

Residual Value—the value as of the end of the discrete projection period in a discounted future earnings model.

Return on Equity—the amount, expressed as a percentage, earned on a company's common equity for a given period.

Return on Investment—See **Return on Invested Capital** and **Return on Equity**.

Return on Invested Capital—the amount, expressed as a percent-age, earned on a company's total capital for a given period.

Risk-Free Rate—the rate of return available in the market on an investment free of default risk.

Risk Premium—a rate of return added to a risk-free rate to reflect risk.

Rule of Thumb—a mathematical formula developed from the relationship between price and certain variables based on experience, observation, hearsay, or a combination of these; usually industry specific.

Special Interest Purchasers—acquirers who believe they can enjoy post-acquisition economies of scale, synergies, or strategic advantages by combining the acquired business interest with their own.

Standard of Value—the identification of the type of value being utilized in a specific engagement; for example, fair market value, fair value, investment value.

Sustaining Capital Reinvestment—the periodic capital outlay required to maintain operations at existing levels, net of the tax shield available from such outlays.

Systematic Risk—the risk that is common to all risky securities and cannot be eliminated through diversification. The measure of systematic risk in stocks is the beta coefficient.

Tangible Assets—physical assets (such as cash, accounts receivable, inventory, property, plant and equipment, etc.).

Terminal Value—See **Residual Value.**

Transaction Method—See **Merger and Acquisition Method**.

Unlevered Beta—the beta reflecting a capital structure without debt.

Unsystematic Risk—the risk specific to an individual security that can be avoided through diversification.

Valuation—the act or process of determining the value of a business, business ownership interest, security, or intangible asset.

Valuation Approach—a general way of determining a value indication of a business, business ownership interest, security, or intangible asset using one or more valuation methods.

Valuation Date—the specific point in time as of which the valuator's opinion of value applies (also referred to as "Effective Date" or "Appraisal Date").

Valuation Method—within approaches, a specific way to determine value.

Valuation Procedure—the act, manner, and technique of performing the steps of an appraisal method.

Valuation Ratio—a fraction in which a value or price serves as the numerator and financial, operating, or physical data serve as the denominator.

Value to the Owner—see **Investment Value.**

Voting Control—de jure control of a business enterprise.

Weighted Average Cost of Capital (WACC)—the cost of capital (discount rate) determined by the weighted average, at market value, of the cost of all financing sources in the business enterprise's capital structure.

Index

A
Accredited Senior Appraiser (ASA), 8
Asset deal, 78
Asset purchase agreement (APA), 85–86

B
Business sale
  APA, 85–86
  asset deal, 78
  asset purchase agreement, 70
  best time and optimal price, 71–72
  business reasons, 79
  CIM, 82
  closing of deal, 86
  confidentiality agreement, 82
  discovery period, 71
  due diligence process, 84, 90
  ESOP, 73–74
  events, 79
  feast-or-famine fee, 69
  financial buyers, 73–74
  housing industry, 70
  LOI, 70, 83
  lucrative fee, 69
  M&A transaction, 89
  reasonable expectation, 89
  retirement forces, 89
  risks, 70
  sales transaction, tax impact
    asset sale, 88
    corporation and individual tax, 88
    M&A transactions, 87
    stock transaction, 87–88
  screening process, 82
  stock deal, 78
  strategy, 75
  success fee, 69
  synergistic buyers, 73
  teaser, 82
  terms of deal
    convenant not to compete, 77
    deal price, 76
    earn-out, 77
    payment, 76
    seller's note, 76
  transaction team selection
    business brokers, 80
    intermediary hire, 81, 89
    investment bankers, 80
    M&A transaction, 81–82
    valuation professionals, 81

C
Compound annual growth rate (CAGR), 61
Confidential information memorandum (CIM), 82
Confidentiality agreement, 82
Country club lifestyle, 1
  compensation, 2
  engagement, 2
  IRS, 1
  nephew, 1
  services and valuation report, 1
  true value, 2

Index

D

Drew's Sensational Snacks
  business operations, 50
  business risk reduction, 56–57, 60
    areas, 60
    rate of return, 61
    risk factors, 57–60
  enterprise value, 50
  facts, 48–49
  growth plan
    CAGR, 61
    net income, 63
    newfound freedom, 64
    organic growth/acquisition, 62
    rate of return, 63
    sustainable growth, 62–63
  hygiene, 50–52
  income statement, 49
  risk concerns, 49–50
  sustainable cash flows
    approaches, 52
    gross margin percentage, 53–54
    operating expenses, 55–56

E, F, G, H

Employee stock ownership plan (ESOP), 73–74

Enterprise value *vs.* equity value, 14

Exit strategy and succession plan, 93–95

I, J, K

Income approaches
  discounted cash flow method, 28–29
  normalization process
    financial statements, 29
    historical earnings, 29–30
    LIFO and FIFO, 30
    owner's compensation issue, 30–31
  single-stream capitalization method, 27
  sustainable cash flow level
    adjustments, 33
    capitalization rate, 34
    convertion, 32
    discount rate, 34
    EBITDA points, 31–32
    enterprise value, 37–38
    rate of return, 34–37
    risk premium, 34
    WACC, 34

Internal Revenue Service (IRS), 1

Investment mindset
  business assets, 3
  Wall Street Journal, 3
  increasing value, 4
  value protection
    action option, 66
    partial list and description, 65

L, M, N, O

Letter of Intent (LOI), 83

P, Q, R

Plan to retire
  inclusions in plan, 93
  items to success, 92

S

Stock deal, 78

T, U

Time for Action. *See* Plan to retire

V

Valuation approaches, 25. *See also* Income approaches
  asset approaches, 40
  divorce cases and shareholder disputes, 25
  equity value
    assumptions, 41
    enterprise value, 41
    financial analysis, 41
    formula, 41
    summary, 41
    value per share, 42–43
  hand-to-hand combat, 26–27
  market approaches
    appraisers, 38
    Guideline Public Company method, 39
    Guideline Transaction method, 40

Valuation fundamentals, 5
  asset approach, 19
  business owners, 5–6

business process, 7
business sale, 69
cash flow, 20
EBITDA, 20
engagement
    asset and stock sale, 15
    date, 17
    enterprise value *vs.* equity value, 14
    factors, 14
    letter, 13
    net proceeds, 15
    purpose, 16
    standards, 15–16
factors
    economic outlook, 18
    historical financial trends, 18
    in-depth understanding, 17
    industry outlook, 18
    IRS Revenue Ruling 17, 59–60
    management forecast, 18
income approach, 19
market approach, 19
plain English-examples
    definitions, 20
    enterprise value, 22
    equity value, 23
    net proceeds, 23–24
    scenario, 22
professionals
    business valuation, 8
    common sense, 9
    credible business valuation, 8–9
    review, 10
    valuator, 9–10
standards
    fair market value, 15–16
    investment value, 15
use of, 10
    have to valuation, 11–12
    should valuation, 12–13
Value growing, 45
    business professionals
        accounting and legal service, 64
        employee manuals and job descriptions, 65
        intangible assets, 66
    business value
        benefits, 47
        goals and plans, 46
        key areas, 47
        strategies, 47–48
    definition, 45
    Drew's newfound freedom, 64
    Drew's Sensational Snacks
        business operations, 50
        business risk reduction, 56–61
        enterprise value, 50
        facts, 48
        gross margin percentage, 53–54
        growth plan, 61–63
        hygiene, 50–52
        income statement, 49
        operating expenses, 55–56
        risk concerns, 49–50
        sustainable cash flows, 52

W, X, Y, Z

Weighted average cost of capital (WACC), 34

Get the eBook for only $10!

Now you can take the weightless companion with you anywhere, anytime. Your purchase of this book entitles you to 3 electronic versions for only $10.

This Apress title will prove so indispensible that you'll want to carry it with you everywhere, which is why we are offering the eBook in 3 formats for only $10 if you have already purchased the print book.

Convenient and fully searchable, the PDF version enables you to easily find and copy code—or perform examples by quickly toggling between instructions and applications. The MOBI format is ideal for your Kindle, while the ePUB can be utilized on a variety of mobile devices.

Go to www.apress.com/promo/tendollars to purchase your companion eBook.

All Apress eBooks are subject to copyright. All rights are reserved by the Publisher, whether the whole or part of the material is concerned, specifically the rights of translation, reprinting, reuse of illustrations, recitation, broadcasting, reproduction on microfilms or in any other physical way, and transmission or information storage and retrieval, electronic adaptation, computer software, or by similar or dissimilar methodology now known or hereafter developed. Exempted from this legal reservation are brief excerpts in connection with reviews or scholarly analysis or material supplied specifically for the purpose of being entered and executed on a computer system, for exclusive use by the purchaser of the work. Duplication of this publication or parts thereof is permitted only under the provisions of the Copyright Law of the Publisher's location, in its current version, and permission for use must always be obtained from Springer. Permissions for use may be obtained through RightsLink at the Copyright Clearance Center. Violations are liable to prosecution under the respective Copyright Law.

Other Apress Business Titles You Will Find Useful

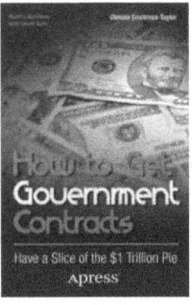

How to Get Government Contracts
Smotrova-Taylor
978-1-4302-4497-4

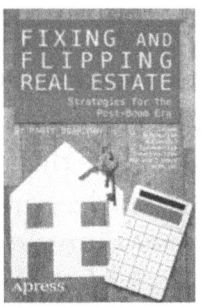

Fixing and Flipping Real Estate
Boardman
978-1-4302-4644-2

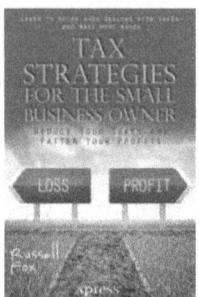

Tax Strategies for the Small Business Owner
Fox
978-1-4302-4842-2

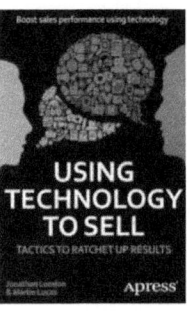

Using Technology to Sell
London
978-1-4302-3933-8

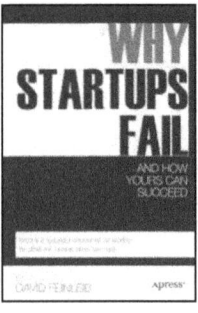

Why Startups Fail
Feinleib
978-1-4302-4140-9

Startup
Ready
978-1-4302-4218-5

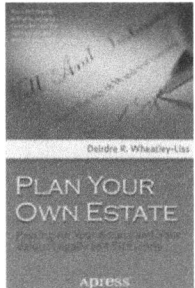

Plan Your Own Estate
Wheatley-Liss
978-1-4302-4494-3

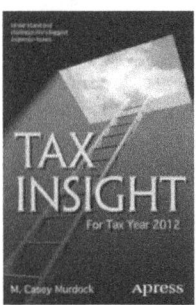

Tax Insight
Casey Murdock
978-1-4302-4737-1

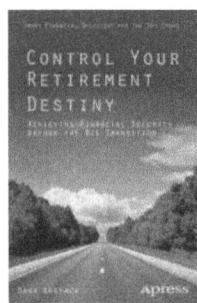

Control Your Retirement Destiny
Dana Anspach
978-1-4302-5002-7

Available at www.apress.com

GPSR Compliance

The European Union's (EU) General Product Safety Regulation (GPSR) is a set of rules that requires consumer products to be safe and our obligations to ensure this.

If you have any concerns about our products, you can contact us on

ProductSafety@springernature.com

In case Publisher is established outside the EU, the EU authorized representative is:

Springer Nature Customer Service Center GmbH
Europaplatz 3
69115 Heidelberg, Germany

www.ingramcontent.com/pod-product-compliance
Lightning Source LLC
LaVergne TN
LVHW040741250326
834688LV00031B/385